Not a Guru

One Woman's Spiritual Journey to Happiness

DESPINA GURLIDES

iUniverse, Inc.
New York Bloomington

Not A Guru

One Woman's Spiritual Journey to Happiness

iUniverse books may be ordered through booksellers or by contacting:

iUniverse
1663 Liberty Drive
Bloomington, IN 47403
www.iuniverse.com
1-800-Authors (1-800-288-4677)

ISBN: 9-781-4401-1244-7 (pbk)
ISBN: 9-781-4401-1245-4 (cloth)
ISBN: 9-781-4401-1246-1 (ebk)

Printed in the United States of America

iUniverse rev. date: 12/15/2008

This book is dedicated to
the only sat-guru there is,
the heart.

With much gratitude to
all the teachers
who have pointed the way Home.

The events in this story are true, though interpreted from my perspective. I do not profess to know what is true for anyone else. Obviously Shangri-La is not the real name of the town I lived in. I named it thus in my book because it seemed to hold the promise, at the time, of the perfect, idyllic place to live. It did not deliver on that promise. The names of the people have been changed, but my cats' names—Max and Bradley—were not.

Prologue

I recently attended a workshop at Esalen called "The Art of Happiness." When the leaders asked, "Who is happy?" I was the only one of forty people who raised my hand. I looked around the room, surprised, as each person told his story of suffering. Since I was the only one claiming to be happy, the workshop leaders asked me for my prescription.

So what is my recipe for happiness? I can give it in a short sentence of four words: *Do NOT betray yourself.*

This is easier said than done. Not betraying yourself means that you do not stay in a loveless marriage just because you don't know how you will pay the bills. You do not stay in a job you hate just because you're earning a hefty six-figure salary. You do not stay in friendships where there is no love and respect just because you've known each other for thirty years. And you do not stay with a spiritual teacher who is condescending and emotionally abusive just because you believe he can offer you enlightenment.

You tell the truth, to yourself and to others, regardless of the consequences, because happiness is a by-product of staying true to yourself. There are no shortcuts. To the extent that your life has been a self-betrayal, you will journey through a dark night of the soul before you can be happy.

This book tells the story of my journey to happiness. Not everyone will relate to my story, but some people will. The people who will relate to Part 1, *Breaking through the Material Trance*, are the ones who have worked their asses off, probably at a prestigious job, and have all the toys they ever wanted. They also have the respect and envy of many people who long to be like them.

Everything in our culture is telling them that they are successful and that they ought to be happy, and yet they are not. They are tired, exhausted, bored, depressed, and stressed out. They long for something, but they don't know what that is. They feel as if they're in prison, despite the fact that they have everyone's admiration.

This book, my story, is here to offer confirmation to these people that they are not crazy, they are not spoiled, they are not greedy. They are in fact in a prison of their own making, because they have listened to society rather than to their hearts.

This book offers the story of my escape from a material prison to a more spiritual life. It shares the joys of that spiritual life and then shows how that too became a prison that I needed to escape from.

The people who will relate to Part 2, *Breaking through the Spiritual Trance,* are the people who have followed a guru, joined a spiritual community, or meditated for years, hoping to become enlightened. Some of them, like me, may have come from a life of extreme materialism. Others may have followed a spiritual path most of their lives, and have never had much money. Regardless, my story will confirm that they are also in a prison of their own making, because they have given their power away to some outside spiritual authority rather than trusting themselves.

My story is not linear, because life is not linear. Rather, events spiral and similar issues come up from a different perspective. I offer what I have learned in the hopes that this serves to support you, wherever you are in your journey.

In the end, no one else can save you. No one knows the truth about how you should live your life. That truth can only be found in your heart, by following your passion and joy. Ultimately, that path leads to your life's work, which is the only true source of happiness.

Despina Gurlides
San Rafael, California

August 2008

Part 1

Breaking Free from the Material Trance

1. Why, if I'm so successful, do I feel so unhappy?

2. When success falls apart,
   important questions arise

3. How can failure be good luck?

4. Depression brings an important message

5. When you take a leap of faith,
   the universe supports you

6. Taking advantage of emptiness

7. Lessons keep repeating themselves
   until you learn them

8. Sometimes you get a short break

9. Facing the bogeyman of bankruptcy

10. The joy of downsizing

11. A spiritual path with four suggestions

12. The dark night of the soul

13. It gets easier to trust the process

14. If your Intention is to be free, you will

    have to meet your worst fear

15. What rewards can failure bring?

    Freedom, joy, fun, rest, purpose!

16. Whatever your talent is, that is the

    work you're meant to be doing

17. Opportunities open up when you

    let go of your baggage

18. A retreat creates the space to meet yourself

19. What do you really want?

20. Recurring dreams have a message

1

Why, if I'm so successful, do I feel so unhappy?

For the first thirty-seven years of my life I tried to fulfill all my desires by becoming successful as it was defined in my world. A first generation Greek born of immigrant parents, I wanted to leave Brooklyn and my ethnic background behind, move to Manhattan, and become sophisticated. I wanted to earn a large salary, have my own credit cards, wear designer clothes, eat at the best restaurants, live in a beautiful apartment, take expensive trips to Europe...and the list went on and on.

I realized I would have to work hard. I would have to be the best student and get scholarships to college and to graduate school since my father couldn't afford to send me and, even if he could, he didn't think that it was needed. My mother was more ambitious for me, insisting that I pursue my education.

But going to graduate school at New York University to obtain an MBA was my idea. I didn't even like business. I liked math and I wanted to teach, but I was aware that teachers earned very small salaries. Furthermore, teaching in public schools in New York City was dangerous; there were often news stories about kids bringing guns to school. I happened to read in *Cosmopolitan* that the new hot degree was an MBA, and that there were very few women who were going for it (this was back in 1975). That seemed like a challenge to me, and I took it on.

To make the business degree more palatable, I majored in Quantitative Analysis, a field as close to pure math as I could get. And I managed to get a scholarship. When I completed my degree, I was able to get a job with a respectable salary. My family was very proud of me, but for me this was just the beginning.

Did I mention that I had been engaged to a Greek man while I lived in Brooklyn? He patiently waited for me to complete my degree so that we could get married. Well, the more I studied, the less he fit in with my idea of success. I broke our engagement midway through graduate school so that I could pursue my dreams unencumbered. Children and a house with a white picket fence were not part of my agenda. They did not lead to the kind of life that I wanted.

I did all the right things to become successful. I stayed in a job for a couple of years, long enough to get some experience, and then moved up to another position with more money and more responsibility. I never left a job without having a job to go to. I dressed in a businesslike style, but kept it just feminine enough that my male bosses would like me and take care of me. The industries that I worked for in the beginning were extremely boring—the container industry and insurance—but that didn't matter as long as they could offer me the salary and the position that I wanted.

As I climbed the corporate ladder, I met a couple of men whom I married. The first marriage lasted only a year, for he soon started talking about children and leaving the city. The second marriage, however, lasted seven years, because it was a good partnership. Michael was brilliant and a good businessman. He was fairly young when I met him but he was going to be very success-ful, and I knew it. He was the perfect man with whom to climb the ladder of success.

At this point you're probably not liking me very much. As I'm writing this, over two decades later, I'm not lik-ing myself either. Where was the passion? Where was the love? Where was the adventure that life can be? Not in this story. My determination to be successful pretty much eliminated all the joy and playfulness from my life. I obtained all the material goods that I had always wanted, and more. I had a great apartment on the Up-per West Side, a summer house in the Hamptons, a big Midtown office with a hefty expense account, a husband who was very successful—and I was bored to death and depressed.

It's really a wonderful gift when you're able to get everything that you've always wanted, not because of the joy of having your desires met (that doesn't last very long), but because you actually find out that those de-sires cannot bring you joy. When you reach that point, you can actually start asking yourself some really impor-tant questions:

- Is success all there is?
- Why, if I'm so successful, do I feel so unhappy?
- What does it take to be happy?
- What is it that I really want?

This last question is the most important question you can ask yourself, and it deserves a chapter all its own.

Usually, when you reach this point—of having achieved success, being unhappy, and asking important questions—your life falls apart. At least mine did. This gave me the space to go inward and get real answers.

2

When success falls apart, important questions arise

It started when Michael left me for another woman. Turns out he wanted a housewife who would have children with him, whereas I was perfectly happy with a business partner. The subsequent divorce woke me up from my successful but boring life. For the first time in my life I felt like a failure. Friends were looking at me in the pitiful way that they look at women who have been dumped. I felt that I had been traded in for a new model. It didn't help that Michael decided to upgrade his car at the same time. I felt like the old car he had replaced.

Failure was thrust upon me and my whole world shattered. The life I had created looked so good on the outside, but Michael's defection totally destroyed the illusion. The truth was that Michael and I weren't happy together, although from the outside our life seemed wonderful. Michael and I never fought, we went to nice restaurants, we had fun shopping together, and we supported each other in our work. However, the marriage was more like a business partnership than a romance, with very little passion and sex. Who had energy for sex, when our whole life force was spent on achieving success?

The marriage ended and I was devastated, not because I loved my husband so much, but because my well-planned life had ended. *What will I do without a summer house?* I remember thinking. It was May, the hot

New York summer was going to start soon, and Michael had gotten the summer house in the settlement.

My marriage was the first failure I experienced, but it was by no means the last. Single again, I threw myself into work because I had nothing else to do, but that started falling apart as well. By this time I was working for a company that sold music and videos through the mail. I had worked my way to the top and was a vice president in the marketing area, running three departments. I had worked for this company for about a decade and the other employees were like a family to me, albeit a dysfunctional family.

There were many perks—such as winter planning meetings in Colorado where we went skiing for ten days—but I was bored with the work. I had worked myself up the ranks with my analytical abilities, which were needed and valued. But there was nothing creative about the work and my boss was emotionally abusive. I couldn't wait for the weekends to come. On Sunday nights I was very depressed because I had to go to work the next day.

What to do? I did the unthinkable. I left a secure high-paying job to join a small company. The change was exciting but the job wasn't. My heart wasn't in it and it showed. Six months later, I left. For the first time since I had started working, I found myself unemployed. I remember going home and standing by the window, still wearing my coat, looking out into Central Park for a couple of hours, frozen in terror.

Who was I, if I wasn't a vice president? I had no business cards. I had no office to go to. I could die tomorrow and no one would even know.

What was I going to do with my time? Everyone in New York was working. The only people I saw on the streets in the middle of a workday were homeless people or nannies with the children they were watching.

What would people think? Would they think that I was a loser? Would I be shunned? Would my mother be upset?

Having lost my identity as Michael's wife, I had now lost my identity as the vice president of the entertainment company. I felt that I had no ground to stand on. I couldn't control any of this.

While this seemed like my worst nightmare at the time, I can tell you in hindsight that it was the best of luck.

3

How can failure be good luck?

For one thing, I finally got to rest. Working in corporate America had left me exhausted—both physically and mentally. Every morning as I crossed the street to take the subway to work, I would see the homeless people sleeping in Central Park and envy them. I envied the fact that they could sleep in—I'm not a morning person. I envied that they didn't have an abusive boss telling them what to do, and criticizing them all the time. I envied that they got to hang out in the park amidst the trees and grass, instead of spending the day in a skyscraper—one of those sick buildings where the windows hadn't opened in three decades.

The truth was that I wasn't only exhausted, I was sick a great deal. For years I thought I had chronic fatigue syndrome and I spent quite a bit of money and time going to doctors, acupuncturists, and other healers, trying to get my energy back. One homeopathic healer, who was quite psychic, told me that I had to quit my job—the building I was working in was making me sick. At the time I thought she was crazy to suggest I leave a job that paid a six-figure salary simply because the building didn't get fresh air. But later I realized she was right. I remembered how sick people had gotten when they first started working in the building, and how they claimed that they never used to get sick. I remembered the headaches that I started having after our floor got new carpeting. I remembered how the air was turned off after six o'clock, even though we were expected to work past that time.

To my surprise, once I stopped working I found that I had a great deal more energy. The chronic fatigue that had been plaguing me for years just disappeared. There were many reasons for this increase in energy. I could sleep in as much as I wanted. I finally was able to rest. Also, once I got over the fear of being unemployed, I really started enjoying myself. I could take walks in Central Park. I could go to bookstores and browse for hours. I could spend the whole day on my couch, reading. I could walk by the movie theater, see that a film was about to start, and buy a ticket on the spur of the moment. Life started to flow in a way it never had before.

When I was working, everything had to be planned, since all my activities happened in the evenings or the weekends when everyone else was out as well. You had to buy movie tickets early or you wound up spending hours in line, especially if it was a new film that had received good reviews. To dine out, you had to make a reservation at the restaurant. In some cases, such as for brunch, you couldn't make reservations. You just had to wait, sometimes for an hour on Sunday, sometimes in the freezing cold on the sidewalk, until your name was called. How great that I could now walk right into my favorite brunch place, Sarabeth's Kitchen, in the middle of the week, without having to wait. *Who*, I asked myself, *were all these people who can eat brunch at eleven o'clock in the middle of the week?* Monday through Fridays, life was actually going on outside of Midtown.

I don't know if I can convey the joy and freedom that I felt while I was unemployed in New York. So I wasn't successful anymore. I could live with that, because what had replaced success was an enjoyment of life. I realized that my energy was coming back not just because I was resting, but also because I was looking forward to each day. When I woke up in the morning, the entire day lay before me like a canvas that I got to paint in any way I chose. I started appreciating the simple pleasures of a good meal, a good book, a stroll through the park, the discovery of a garden, a chat with a stranger. My busy schedule had never really allowed me the time and space to enjoy everyday life.

One Sunday night I started to get depressed. The Sunday night blues were something that I knew well. They had visited me every week for decades, whenever I started to think about having to go to work the next day. Then it occurred to me there was nothing to be depressed about—I wasn't going to work on Monday. And the Sunday blues left. I wish that I could say that I was never visited by depression again, but that wouldn't be true. Depression came—deep, dark depression. And like failure, depression was also a friend visiting me with an important message.

4

Depression brings an important message

For me, depression is always a sign that something is not working in my life. Something needs to change—and it's usually something so big that I can't acknowledge it because that would mean the end of life as I know it. It's unfortunate that so many people take medication to alleviate the symptom of depression. The medication may keep them functional and successful, but it doesn't heal the source of the depression. Luckily for me, I don't believe in taking any drugs. I don't even take an aspirin when I get a headache.

When I was first divorced, I went to a doctor for some mild illness. He pulled out my file and asked if anything had changed since he had last seen me. When I told him that I had recently been divorced, he tried to give me antidepressants. I wasn't even depressed at the time. Of course I didn't take them, but I was amazed at how easily some doctors prescribe antidepressants—even when you don't ask for them.

When I'm depressed, I let myself be depressed. I feel the darkness, the emptiness, the hopelessness. What's the big deal? They're just feelings. When the feelings settle down, I can tell myself the truth about why I'm depressed. There is always a reason. After enjoying several months of freedom, enjoying my life of unemployment, something changed. I was starting to get bored. It was time to work again. Another chapter of my life was beginning.

I put my résumé together, contacted the headhunters, and started interviewing for a job. My résumé was really good and I interview well, so I didn't anticipate any problems, but I had been away from the business world too long. I had tasted sanity and it was impossible to go back to the success paradigm. One of the vice presidents I interviewed with was a workaholic who told me proudly that his last vacation had been seventeen years ago on his honeymoon. Another woman in Human Resources told me that she worked twenty-four/seven. Even if I had the energy to work that hard, I could no longer buy into their belief that working was the only priority in life. I began to question whether I could work in the business world at all.

That wasn't a surprise. What was surprising was that I began to question whether I could still live in New York. You have to understand that I am a born and bred New Yorker. Like most New Yorkers, I used to feel that the entire world revolved around New York City. Whenever I left New York, even if it was to go on a great Caribbean vacation, the sight of the city would bring tears to my eyes when I returned. Before I married my two husbands, I had a talk with each of them. I told them that there were two things that I would never do: I would never have children and I would never leave New York. At least I stuck with one of these.

But here I was, done with New York. I had spent six months totally enjoying the City, but now summer had come—hot and humid summer—and I didn't have a summer house to go to. Not only that, my beautiful apartment only had air conditioning in the bedroom. Michael and I hadn't wanted to ruin the views outside our picture windows by installing it. It hadn't been a big problem when we worked during the day and went away on the weekends, but now I was stuck in the apartment with no air-conditioned office to go to and no beach house. Walking through Central Park in the heat and the humidity had lost its appeal. I was also tired of being alone. My friends were either working or going on vacation and had little time for me. In a city where everyone has so little time, I found that I had too much. With nothing to do and nowhere to go, each second felt like an hour. The heat and eternity really felt like hell.

And so depression came. A depression so dark that I wished I were dead. Death—another state that people avoid thinking about, which also can be a friend. As I sat in my living room one evening feeling death would be a much better alternative than the life I was leading, I pretended that I had died. I began to think of everything I would be leaving behind: my friends and family, my cats, my apartment, my clothes, my body, my experiences…the list went on and on. When I was through, it occurred to me that if I was willing to die and lose all that, then perhaps I could do something less drastic. Perhaps I could leave New York. Sure, I would have to leave my friends and family and the beautiful co-op apartment that I owned. But at least I would get to keep my cats, my body, my clothes, and a whole bunch of other good stuff. If I was willing to die, well, I could move to California instead. The idea of death allowed me to let go and open up to new possibilities. The message depression was sending me was that it was time to leave New York.

5

When you take a leap of faith, the universe supports you

After my divorce I started asking questions about who I was and what my purpose was. Many of the books that I read in my free time were metaphysical, describing ideas that felt true to me. Simple ideas such as, "Our thoughts create our reality," which I take for granted now, at the time seemed profound. I had begun exploring various aspects of metaphysics, including channeling and shamanism. These all served to connect me with realms beyond the material world, and to connect me with the magic that is life.

Channeling, shamanism—these were things I didn't discuss with my New York acquaintances. I didn't want them to think I was weird. I was a closet metaphysician. *How great it would be*, I thought, *if I lived in a place where these things were more acceptable*. Marin was that place. And it was still very close to a cool, sophisticated city. I wouldn't miss New York with San Francisco just twenty minutes away.

For the most part, leaving New York was one of the most magical experiences I have had. Everything went smoothly and easily. It was as if the entire universe conspired to help me. I have since found out that when you follow your heart and take a leap of faith, even if—or especially if—you are frightened, everything comes together to support you. Synchronicities happen that leave you with your mouth open. People show up who help you in ways you couldn't imagine. Almost as soon as you think of something that you need, it manifests. The world is no longer a humdrum place where you have to plan, control, and do everything on your own. The world becomes a magical place where you put in your order and watch with curiosity and amazement as it is delivered.

Let me get more specific. The first thing I had to do was sell my beautiful co-op. I had run out of money after living off of my savings for six months. I sat down on the couch with a pen and a pad of paper and figured out the amount I would like to net from the sale. I also decided I would like my neighbor to sell it. He was a sweet man who had been a house husband, had raised his daughter, and now had entered the business world by becoming a realtor. He was a gentle soul and I was concerned that more experienced realtors would eat him alive. He hadn't closed a deal yet, and I wanted to give him my apartment so he could prove himself.

He was grateful to have the listing at a time when classic-six prewar apartments were scarce. However, he—and everyone else in the building—thought I was asking for too much money—fifty thousand dollars more than any other price brought by an apartment in the same line. I didn't budge. We had put a lot of work in the apartment. It had a huge, beautiful eat-in kitchen, and it was on the seventeenth floor with incredible city views and partial park views. The apartment would sell. Not only would it sell, but I knew that the people who would buy it would love it. I couldn't imagine my apartment going to someone who wanted it just for an investment; it was my home. Sure enough, within a couple of weeks my friend the realtor got an offer from a couple who had fallen in love with the apartment. They offered the exact amount I had written on my pad and they were willing to wait three months, until January, to close. This would give me enough time to find a place to live in California, to pack, to spend the Christmas holidays in New York, and to start my new life in January of 1997.

I had decided to move to Marin County, which is just north of San Francisco over the Golden Gate Bridge. I had recently heard about Marin from a few friends. It sounded like Shangri-La: a beautiful place with good restaurants and a lot of wealthy people who didn't seem to work. Marin also had the added bonus of being a spiritual place where I could explore various aspects of my newfound spirituality.

Not knowing how to drive was a bit of a hindrance, but that didn't stop me. I found a friend, Dwight, who was willing to go with me to Marin and drive around as I looked for a place to live. It was October, a time when New Yorkers are already feeling the cool, chilly autumn, but when we arrived in Marin, to my delight, it still felt like summer. In Mill Valley people were sitting outside at the café, chatting and enjoying the warmth. Tall trees that I hadn't seen before, redwoods, formed circular sanctuaries in the park nearby. And I thought Central Park was the epitome of nature!

We went to a wonderful grocery store, Whole Foods, with great organic produce and tasty prepared foods, which made my little health food store on the Upper West Side seem meager in comparison. To my surprise, the cashier actually smiled and chatted with us as she rang up the groceries, instead of throwing the change back. When a realtor showed me a three bedroom house to rent—with a deck and garden—for the price of a tiny studio apartment in Manhattan, I was sold. Mill Valley was the place for me.

6

Taking advantage of emptiness

Mill Valley was everything I thought it would be. I felt as if I were Mary Poppins, entering a painting of the perfect town: happy dogs playing in the town center, happy people chatting over their café lattes, beautiful blonde babies with their beautiful blonde mothers strolling down the sidewalks. I wound up renting a cottage in the woods that was within walking distance of the downtown area. It had to be walking distance, since I still didn't know how to drive.

I started taking driving lessons but I was in no hurry to have a car. Life became really simple. I walked into town, sat at the café, chatted with people, and took walks by the creek. I joined a little gym. I had a key and could pretty much unlock the door and work out whenever I wanted. After living in New York City most of my life, I found life in this small town enchanting. OK, I had some tasks such as finding the right hair cutter and hair colorist. And at some point I would have to look for work. But the sale of my apartment had given me a really nice nest egg so there was no rush.

In the beginning it didn't seem to bother me much that I didn't know anyone. I was enjoying the novelty, and for companionship I had long telephone conversations with friends and family in New York. As I settled in, though, I found that the aloneness was deep. I felt like a hermit. I wondered how many people could live the way I was living: no family, no friends, no relationship, no work. I found myself in a place that I call "nothing." It's a place that many people don't get to visit—certainly not many people in New York. And yet it's a place that is necessary if you are on a spiritual path because you get to find out who you are. Without the busy-ness and the social interactions, space is created for you to meet yourself—to meet your hopes, but most importantly, to meet your deepest, darkest fears.

Some days I didn't think I could make it. Fears of being alone, of being abandoned, of being unloved, of not existing—all came to visit. I didn't feel as if I would ever have a normal life again, a life that involved work, dating, going out with friends. Of all circumstances, I think emptiness is the most challenging. It's very close to death. That's probably why most people avoid it like the plague.

One thing I'm learning is that life is like breathing. You have to inhale and exhale; you have to go inward and then outward. Emptiness is like the pause between the two. I find that I have caused myself unnecessary suffering by complaining when the emptiness appears, instead of taking advantage of it and resting. A part of me doesn't trust that it will all be OK, that I'm just going through a stage that will end. Part of me still thinks I have to control the outcome—I have to get aggressive and make changes happen. The truth is that changes happen on their own. If it's time to be inward, take advantage of it: rest and get to know yourself. Eventually the energy will shift and you will find that you are in an outward mode, dealing with the world, working, and making your contribution.

The time came for me to be "outward" in Marin. A headhunter contacted me about work. The owner of an ad agency in Portrero Hill had seen my résumé and was very interested in me. The ad agency was a very good creative shop but they wanted an analytical nerd like me to head up a department to do marketing analysis for their clients. Managing the marketing strategy of a client made it unlikely that the client would leave.

I drove to Portrero Hill, which was about an hour away during rush hour, and had a great interview. The building was very cool—a converted soap factory that had been redesigned with lots of bright colors. The people were very cool also—almost all of them under forty. The environment seemed like fun. I was offered a great office and a six-figure salary, and I accepted. I was seduced back into the business world. *This will be different*, I thought. *The business world in San Francisco is much more fun and humane than the business world in New York.* That's what I told myself, even as I began recreating the life I had had in New York.

7

Lessons keep repeating themselves until you learn them

What I have learned is that lessons keep repeating themselves. You may think that you have passed a test but the same test shows up again, in a different form, from a different perspective. I see life as a spiral. You may have visited a certain area but you get to revisit it later on from a deeper perspective.

I thought that I had passed the test of not selling out for money. I was very proud of myself for leaving the entertainment company—which was safe but boring—for leaving the next company even though I didn't have a job, for saying *no* when interviews showed up for positions that I knew I would not enjoy. I was really proud of myself for leaving New York behind and heading West to a new adventure. I thought that everything had changed.

Yet, once again, I found myself in a job that was exhausting. I had an hour commute and had to wake up at six o'clock every morning to go to work (did I mention that I'm not a morning person?). I was expected to work until late into the night if a client presentation was coming up (something was always coming up). Every morning I would be deluged with e-mails about meetings that were going to happen that day. There could be seven or eight meetings a day, each meeting going on and on, without an agenda and without someone to lead it in a professional manner.

"Professional" was something that this advertising agency was still working on. I could see why it was such a creative shop. The employees were like children run amok in kindergarten, crayons in hand, creating beautiful work. Few employees controlled their emotions; entry level people were screaming at the vice presidents. Whatever happened to the hierarchy? Business in New York may have been boring but at least there were rules that everyone knew and followed. Here there were no rules—just chaos. There was no time to think; everyone was too busy running around. It could have been the bright colors of the rooms or it could have been the caffeine, but people seemed to be on speed. No wonder most of the employees were in their twenties or early thirties. After that, they burned out.

The owner of the agency was an emotional man who took it personally when employees resigned. People leaving the agency were *personae non gratae*; employees couldn't associate with them or they would be considered disloyal. I imagined the human resources manager to be a spy, cajoling people to tell her their secrets and then passing all the information to her boss. In my more paranoid moments I imagined she tapped the phones and reviewed our e-mails.

There were, of course, benefits for putting up with this craziness. In the summer, the company rented houseboats on Shasta Lake and the entire company—about seventy people—got to party for about a week. We went to expensive dinners with the clients at cool restaurants in San Francisco. We visited winery clients in Napa, and took first-class trips to New York to meet with East Coast clients.

But I wasn't happy. Every morning when the alarm clock rang I sat in bed for half an hour, wishing that I didn't have to go into the office. The Sunday night blues made their reappearance, except I could call them the Sunday night reds. I wasn't just depressed thinking about going into work the next day, I was in deep despair, feeling hopeless, as if I had been incarcerated in an insane asylum. Once again I longed to sleep late, rest, take walks through the woods, and not have to answer to a boss. How did I get here? But maybe this time I didn't have to be unemployed. Many people in California were self-employed, doing consulting. The Internet industry was booming. Perhaps I could cash in on that ...

8

Sometimes you get a short break

And so I tried to cash in on the Internet industry. Why not? Everyone else was doing it. Perhaps I could make some big bucks.

I can't say that this industry really appealed to me. I had never been a high-tech person. As a matter of fact, I had just learned to use computers and the Internet when I moved to California. In New York I had had a secretary who did all the typing. I wrote my memos by hand on a pad of paper, she typed them, and then I made corrections. The people who worked for me used computers to perform heavy-duty analyses that I would review, but I never had to get on a computer myself.

Well, it was time to join the twentieth century. If I could learn to drive, I could learn to work with computers. And I did. But I never became enamored with them and to this day I like keeping a paper calendar. I like writing my appointments in pencil and erasing them when they're canceled. I like reading hard copies. I prefer to search through the phone book when I need a certain service and then call on the phone, rather than search the Internet.

But I was willing to work in the Internet industry if it meant earning a lot of money. I had over fifteen years of direct marketing experience which I thought Internet companies could benefit from. After all, the Internet was essentially a direct marketing tool, but no one working for

Internet companies seemed to have a direct marketing background. Rather than learning from an established industry, it seemed to me that the Internet industry was reinventing the wheel. It didn't help that most of the CEOs were in their mid-twenties. I was surprised to see how young they were. What was even more surprising was talking to them about how I could improve profitability. It seemed that profits weren't important to these people; something called clicks were important. I felt as if I were Alice in Wonderland. How could an industry that didn't care about profits survive? What was I missing?

I kept searching for clients who might understand the importance of profit. I finally found one. The CEO was a man in his forties. What a relief. He even had a direct marketing background and understood the importance of having someone with experience work for him. I was in heaven. It helped that I was being paid eighteen thousand dollars a month in consulting fees to work four days a week, one of which was from home. The days were normal nine to five days without any late hours. I didn't really have any responsibility. My job was to support the CEO and the vice president of marketing with analyses that would be used to develop the marketing strategy.

I have to say that I really enjoyed my life for the short four-month period that I worked for this company. The office was in downtown San Francisco. I could take the ferry from Sausalito. What a change from riding the New York subways. I would sit in the ferry, have coffee and a doughnut, chat with other people, and look at the gorgeous scenery going by—the Golden Gate Bridge, Alcatraz, San Francisco from a distance. The office was a short walk from the ferry. It took up an entire floor in a loft-like building, and I didn't mind that there were no private offices because I enjoyed working in the open and chatting with intelligent, enthusiastic employees who were half my age.

The only distressing aspect of my job was the analysis. The good news was that, for the first time, the CEO and vice president had the information they needed to make their marketing decisions. The bad news was that I couldn't figure out how they were staying afloat. Their costs were way too high and their income was way too low. As it turned out, they weren't. Four months after I started working for them, the doors closed. The whole Internet industry crashed, and so did my high lifestyle.

My accountant still laughs when she remembers me telling her that I couldn't live on eighteen thousand dollars a month. I needed more money. Somehow I thought my income would just keep increasing and I would always be able to get a job when I needed one. I was wrong.

9

Facing the bogeyman of bankruptcy

I never thought my money would run out. I never thought I would have financial difficulties. I had done all the right things. I studied hard and attended good schools. I worked my way to the top. I had an impressive two-page résumé, I knew how to dress for success, and I always did well on interviews. Of course I would get another job. Only losers were unemployed—people who didn't bother going to school, who didn't have the right work ethic, who weren't that smart, who didn't have good social skills.

What arrogance. It's amazing that arrogance is an advantage in the business world. It is confused with self-confidence, but it's not the same thing at all. Arrogance is condescending, rating other people according to their success and dismissing those who are deemed unworthy, never seeing them for who they are. I am so sorry for all the pain my arrogance has caused to others—and to myself as well.

Being unemployed had not been a problem in the past. First I had had my savings to fall back on. Then I cashed out my 401K. Then I sold my Manhattan apartment, which provided me with a nice nest egg of three hundred thousand dollars. That was a lot of money and I never imagined it could run out. But it had.

I had been maintaining the lifestyle that I had when I was married to Michael. I had moved to a three bedroom house in Mill Valley, had a car, ate out at restaurants all the time (I don't cook), took lots of trips back to New York (mostly to get a good haircut as I hadn't found a stylist whom I liked in Marin), bought a whole new wardrobe (my New York clothes were too businesslike and not cool enough for San Francisco), and worked only sporadically for quite a few years. Marin County is an expensive place to live; only a New Yorker would consider it inexpensive. The money was definitely dwindling.

Desperately I looked for work in an economy that had crashed. There was none. I went through my entire nest egg. Still there was no work. I tapped into my IRA until it ran out. Finally I started living off of credit cards, hoping that the high-paying job would show up. I had two credit cards with twenty-five thousand dollar credit limits and I kept getting offers for new credit cards, with 0% interest. I started moving money around, getting a new credit card to pay off the old one, because the interest was killing me. I finally found myself with a hundred thousand dollars in credit card debt.

My accountant told me it was time to declare bankruptcy. The high-paying job wasn't showing up and I couldn't sustain the debt I had. Bankruptcy! That sounded like death to me. I had always had an excellent credit rating, paying all my bills on time. Here was another identity that was falling away from me. Although failure had been visiting me since my divorce, I felt as if we were now getting married. The whole world would know what a failure I was.

It's interesting that when you meet the terrifying bogeyman face to face, it's never as scary as you imagined. For years I had been terrified of going bankrupt, trying to avoid it at all costs. But when the time finally came, it was almost a relief. Most of the suffering happens when you're resisting something. Acceptance brings relief.

OK, I would file bankruptcy. I found a lawyer who consoled me by telling me that I was in good company. Many successful people were now declaring bankruptcy. I have to admit that made me feel better. I filed the papers and went to court on the appointed date. To my surprise the hearing only took a couple of minutes. When the judge heard that I had worked for the Internet industry, he didn't have any questions. The bankruptcy was approved and I felt much lighter. The hundred thousand dollars in debt had felt very heavy indeed.

10

The joy of downsizing

I lightened up by getting rid of my debt, but I needed to lighten up even more. The house I was renting cost three thousand dollars a month and I could no longer afford it. Besides, why did I, one person, need a house with three bedrooms, a huge living room, a formal dining room, and a large eat-in kitchen? I never cooked. I never gave large dinner parties. One bedroom was set up as an office but I no longer had any work to do. Another bedroom was a guest room but I rarely had guests.

It was a beautiful home, well decorated with lots of expensive furniture, rugs, prints, and plants. I had spent thousands of dollars over the years buying all the stuff that was in my house. I liked looking at it. I liked showing my home off to the few people who visited. But what was this home really costing me?

It wasn't just costing me three thousand dollars a month. It was costing me my life. Whether I liked the work or not, I had to find a job that paid me a six-figure salary so that I could maintain a house large enough to put all my stuff in it. I was stressed out about finding work to support my stuff. Then I had a revelation. What if I downsized and moved to a cheaper place? What if I sold or gave away some of my stuff? What if I simplified my life so that I didn't need to find a high-powered job to support myself? What if my focus changed from being successful to being happy?

Since I wasn't working in San Francisco I didn't need to live within commuting distance of the city. I could find a cheaper house deeper in Marin. I began to look for rentals in towns such as San Rafael, San Anselmo, and Fairfax, but found that they weren't much cheaper than Mill Valley. I really needed a dramatic decrease in my expenses. I had hoped I could continue to live by myself, as I had never had a housemate and didn't really want one, but finally I acknowledged that perhaps a housemate wasn't such a bad idea.

As soon as I became open to the idea of sharing a house, a housemate appeared. On a rainy Sunday I found myself looking at a big house in Fairfax. It was a duplex, perfectly laid out for sharing with one bedroom and bathroom downstairs and another set upstairs. Another woman was also looking to rent and we began talking. The house was beautiful and bigger than either of us needed, but it would be perfect for us to share. Moving in with her was taking a leap, but my rent would be halved.

Once we decided to move in together, everything went smoothly. Martha and I agreed what furniture we would each bring, and I was able to sell the rugs and furniture I wasn't taking with me. The house was also nicer than the one I had rented in Mill Valley. It felt as if it were in the countryside, neighboring on a hill where deer came up to our windows. A beautiful trail started at our front door, and yet we were only a five-minute walk from downtown Fairfax—a charming, earthy, slightly offbeat town with a great health food store, good restaurants, and music clubs at night.

Adjusting to having a housemate was challenging. I had to learn about compromising and considering someone else in my plans. It felt a little restrictive, but it was good medicine for someone used to calling all the shots.

I settled into my new home and I really loved it. With my expenses halved, I thought I would be able to find a way to support myself. Perhaps I could make enough money by tutoring math. I had always wanted to teach and after all, I only needed an annual income of about sixty thousand dollars. That was peanuts compared to what I used to make. *Of course things are going to work out,* I thought. *They have to.*

But to my surprise, I lived in Fairfax for only seven months. The sixty thousand dollar job never showed up. I hadn't downsized enough. How much lower could I go? Would I be homeless? That had always been my worst fear. This fear paralyzed me. I didn't know what to do. I had never been religious, but I started praying for help.

Fortunately, my prayers were answered.

11

A spiritual path with four suggestions

One night I was sitting in my living room channel surfing when I saw a smiling man on the local cable access television channel. I wasn't in a good mental place at the time. I couldn't find work and I didn't know what to do. I was paralyzed with fear. When I'm this afraid I tend to numb out by watching a lot of TV and eating a lot of chocolate. That's what I was doing this night. There were about twenty candy wrappers on the coffee table—how could I have eaten that much chocolate?—and I was watching a *Star Trek* episode. The show broke for a commercial and, since I have no patience for commercials, I started to flip through the channels.

At the cable access channel I stopped out of curiosity. I had to know why this man was smiling—smiling in a way that I had never seen before. I later found out that this was Jacob, a spiritual teacher. He did look a little like the Buddha, I thought. But what was he doing?

A woman asked him a question and Jacob's expression changed. The loving smile was replaced with an intense look as he asked the woman: "What do you really want?" She was complaining about not liking her job but staying for the money. "What do you really want?" he asked again. "If you only had one wish, what would it be?"

Jacob went on to tell a story of donkeyhood. Most people go through life as donkeys do: they run away from the stick and run towards the carrot. Most of us spend our time running away from our fears and running towards our desires. The story got my attention; I certainly had spent my life doing that. My biggest fear was not having money and I had done everything in my power to make sure that I had it. And with this money I chased so many desires, but none of them brought me happiness.

Jacob pointed to the possibility of stopping acting like a donkey. What if you turned around and met your fears? What if you didn't move towards your desires? The possibility was to break out of the life of a donkey—a life of suffering—and instead live a life of freedom. This was the way Home. It was pretty simple. You had to combine all of your desires into one desire: the desire for freedom, for truth, for awakening.

My mind didn't understand everything he said, but my heart did. I knew that I was hearing Truth with a capital T. It was very simple, really. All you had to do was:

1. *Tell the truth, always.* Not just tell the truth to others. It was even more important to tell the truth to yourself. The truth was that I hated working in the business world and I only did it for the money and the prestige. The truth was that I really wanted to rest; I didn't want to work. The truth was that I was tired of the rat race.

2. *Stop telling your story.* We all like to talk about ourselves, analyze things, discuss how we've been hurt, talk about our wounds. What if we didn't spend our energy doing that? What if I stopped telling my story of how my husband left me, how I went through all my money, how I couldn't find a

job, how afraid I was of becoming homeless?

3. *Meet what's here.* What if I didn't spend my time rehashing the past or worrying about the future? What if I just felt the fear? The interesting thing is that the fear dissipated when I just felt it instead of trying to suppress it or indulging in expressing it.

4. *Find out who you really are.* One by one many of my identities had dropped away. I was no longer the wife or the successful businesswoman. So who was I really, at the deepest level? What was it about me that never changed?

This is how a New York woman of Greek descent, with an MBA and over twenty years of business experience, met her spiritual teacher. I had never been interested in Indian philosophies and I had never aspired to having a guru. I didn't even know what a guru was, apart from reading some horror stories about cults and unsavory sexual practices. So I wasn't prepared to feel joy and love while listening to a stranger on TV for an hour. But in that hour my life opened up to a possibility that I had never imagined—the possibility that I could wake up in this lifetime and end my suffering.

12

The dark night of the soul

Turning points, at least mine, often involve a descent into the dark night of the soul. What is the dark night of the soul? It's going deep into your psyche and dredging up your worst nightmares so that you can meet them. The gate to freedom, I've heard Jacob say, is guarded by death and terror. When I first heard him say that, I thought he was exaggerating. I later realized that he was dead serious.

We each have our own version of hell. For some people it's losing an intimate relationship. For others it's losing their family or community. For some it's losing their power or health. For me it was losing my money and my stuff. Even when I was married to the investment banker and I had my own six-figure income, I had always had the fear of being homeless. Friends to whom I confided this would laugh. I had so much. How could I ever be homeless?

It's amazing how quickly you can go through money—your 401 K, your savings, your IRA, your credit cards. All the buffers you've set up to keep you secure can disappear quite easily. Truly, there is no such thing as security—at least not security that comes from external things.

So here I was, living in Fairfax with a housemate, downsized, bankrupt, and with no job. The San Francisco Bay Area economy had crashed. I had gone through all my money sources. Both my sister and mother had loaned me money, which they didn't think they would see again. (I'm happy to report that I have paid my mother back and am in the process of paying back my sister.) To make matters worse, my housemate found a beautiful little house to buy and she moved out. Now I was responsible for the entire rent and I couldn't handle it. I would have to move again, but where and how?

I was so terrified I didn't know what to do. I spent days in bed unable to get up because I was paralyzed with fear. I thought of killing myself but I was too much of a coward. In hindsight it seems ridiculous, but at the time I felt as if suicide was my only option. I wouldn't have to deal with the shame and embarrassment of not being able to pay my rent and my other bills, of being a woman in her forties with no funds. My mother, who is very connected to me, felt that something was wrong and she called me every couple of hours to make sure I was OK. I wouldn't answer her calls because I couldn't bear to talk with anyone, but I sent her e-mails so she would leave me alone.

My mother invited me to move in with her. She is one of those wonderful Greek mothers who love to cook, clean, and garden, and she loves having her children around. She suggested that I sell all my furniture, take the two cats, and move. It sounded so easy and I would have felt so safe. But she lives in Florida and I don't like Florida. I loved California. My friends were in California and so was my teacher. What would I do in Florida?

Though I decided I couldn't take her up on her offer, her suggestion helped me see that I could be much freer if I gave up my stuff. Hadn't I decided that I wanted freedom? I still had way too much furniture: a Duxiana bed that cost five thousand dollars, a Henry Miller ergonomic office chair that cost a thousand dollars, and on and on. Why did I need all this stuff? What if I kept only the few things that I really loved? I could move into a room and pay very little rent. What a relief that would be!

I went into a meditation to try to get perspective. I saw a huge gate, the gate to Freedom. I was on the outside but Jacob was with me and he took my hand. Two black-hooded figures stood on each side of the gate. I knew that one was Death and the other Terror, but I was willing to go through the gate. The gate opened and I saw a huge courtyard with a bonfire in the middle. I heard Jacob's voice asking me, "What are you not willing to give for Freedom?" One by one I threw all my possessions into the bonfire. It seemed ridiculous to hold onto anything when Freedom was at stake. In the end I jumped into the fire myself and I let it take me.

I woke up with a very different attitude, feeling as if my life was just beginning. I had decided to sell or give away most of my things and, to my surprise, I felt great. I hadn't realized what a weight I had been carrying. Every time I moved I had to spend weeks packing all the knick-knacks. I had to maintain an expensive house to show off my things. I had to work at an abusive job to maintain the house. What a relief to let it all go. I couldn't wait to begin.

And the entire universe, it seemed, showed up to support me.

13

It gets easier to trust the process

As soon as I decided to sell my things, people showed up to help me. It was another one of those times when magic happened, similar to my move to Mill Valley. Since I already had experienced the support that comes when you take a leap of faith dictated by your heart, I was able to trust the process more.

Ellen, a friend of a friend, was not working at the time and she offered to throw a garage sale for me. She also had several friends who were interior decorators; they came to my house and bought the expensive things. My landlady fell in love with some of the artwork and purchased it at the price I had originally paid. Girlfriends showed up to buy La Perla lingerie that had never been worn. Each day felt like a party. I was happy to be building up some equity—or at least enough money to move— and my friends were happy because they were getting great bargains on things they loved.

It was an unusually hot July in Marin. In addition, I was experiencing hot flashes (yep, not only did I not have money, but I was also menopausal). I made a list of all the things that needed to be done that month. Let's see…I needed to find a new place to live. I needed to sell most of my possessions. I needed to pack and move. I was planning to attend a ten-day retreat at Harbin Hot Springs—not to mention that a couple of friends were visiting me from Europe before the retreat, and three friends wanted to visit me from Connecticut at the end of July, just when I was suppose to move.

I had also just been hired to tutor two girls. One was an Olympic skier to whom I would be teaching pre-calculus every day so that she could complete the course in the summer. In the winter she would be busy skiing. Another student was taking probability and statistics at the College of Marin. Even though I had been a math major, I hadn't seen pre-calculus or statistics in at least two decades. But I couldn't turn down work so I was going to study and keep one chapter ahead of my students.

How was I going to get all of this accomplished in one month? My mind, so good at planning, couldn't figure it out. Every time it tried to think about everything that needed to be done, it short-circuited. This was the first time that had ever happened to me.

There was something very good about this. For the first time in my life I was able to get out of my head and not think about the future. The future was so unknown and it was so clear that I had no control over it, that I had to surrender. The only way I could function was by staying in the present and doing what showed up in the moment. This worked. I focused on one thing at a time and when that was done, the next thing showed up. I would be meeting with one person and as soon as he or she left, the phone would ring and it would be the next person I needed to deal with. It was as if I had the perfect secretary to schedule my appointments with impeccable timing.

One of the most important realizations was that I was not in control. *Really.* Someone else was writing the screenplay of my life and I was just the actor, meeting whatever showed up to the best of my abilities. This was very good news indeed. I could finally relax because

I wasn't the one who had to plan everything. A higher power was doing the planning and it was so much more creative than anything my small mind could have come up with.

I found a great room in a charming hundred-year old house in Gerstle Park, one of the nicest neighborhoods in Marin. My visiting friends from Connecticut offered to rent a U-Haul and move me. It was the easiest and certainly cheapest move I had ever made. I re-learned my math pretty quickly and developed an intimate relationship with my students. This was the beginning of a lucrative tutoring career. And I had a wonderful ten-day retreat at Harbin Hot Springs with Jacob and about eighty of my closest friends. I will always remember that July as the month when the impossible became possible.

The dark night had lifted and I could see the dawn. My new life was starting. But first I had to experience my worst fear, if only for one night.

14

If your intention is to be free, you will have to meet your worst fear

One thing I have learned is that if there is something that you are really afraid of—if you feel you can handle anything but *that*—you will have to meet that fear at some point in your life, if your intention is to be free. Otherwise that fear will keep you a slave because you will be willing to do anything—even betray yourself—to avoid it. Once you meet that fear it will no longer have the hold over you that it once did.

My greatest fear was being homeless. I had to feel what being homeless was like so that I could be free of that fear. This doesn't mean that I had to be homeless for years. For me, one night was enough. I felt the energy and I saw that it wasn't that bad. Actually, you can meet whatever fear you have in a few minutes if you are willing to stop and really feel it. That would be the conscious way of doing it.

In my case, I created it subconsciously. It was the day that I was moving to my new home in Gerstle Park. My friends packed all of my belongings from Fairfax and drove the U-Haul the short ten minutes to my new home. They unpacked me and then we went to dinner. My new housemate, Harvey, had been present during the unpacking but he decided to spend the night at his girlfriend's house so I would have the place to myself.

This way I could unpack until the wee hours of the night without disturbing him.

After dinner at the Royal Thai, my favorite Thai restaurant in Marin, I came home to a room full of boxes and my two cats, Max and Bradley. I spent the next four hours unpacking. First I took care of my boys by setting up their food and litter box so they could feel at home. Then I unpacked the clothes and put them in my closet. Finally I made the bed.

It was midnight and I was feeling pretty grungy. I had been wearing old clothes for the move and after hours of manual labor in the heat I was in desperate need of a bath. I couldn't wait to take a shower and get into my comfy bed (the Duxiana bed was one of the few things I kept). I had just one cardboard box to throw out. I rushed out the front door to put the box on the porch and heard the door click behind me. Oh, shit! I had locked myself out.

The cats looked at me from the window inside, wondering why I wasn't coming back in. It was midnight. I didn't have a phone and even if I had, I didn't know Harvey's girlfriend's phone number. Desperately I looked for a spare key under every flower pot but I couldn't find one. Finally I decided I would have to sleep on the porch and hope that Harvey would come home in the morning before he went to work. The good news was that it was a clear night in July, there was a futon on the porch, and the neighborhood felt very safe.

I curled up on the futon hoping I could fall asleep, but the wind started blowing. Evenings in Marin are always cool even when the days are hot. I was wearing shorts and a T-shirt, and soon I was cold. I looked around to see if there were any neighbors I could ask for help, but everyone seemed to be sleeping. The windows were dark, except for one window in a complex of condominium apartments.

I couldn't imagine knocking on a stranger's door in the middle of the night to ask for help, but I was desperate. I took a deep breath and knocked on the door. A man opened it, wearing only pajama bottoms, and looked at me questioningly. I could see myself through his eyes— an unwashed, poorly dressed woman, shivering in the cold—but I was too cold to be embarrassed. I explained what had happened and that I would have to sleep outside. Could I borrow a blanket or a sleeping bag? He seemed careful but kind. Why, he asked, hadn't I broken a window to get back in? The thought hadn't occurred to me, but the windows were vintage and I knew my new housemate would be very upset with me if I started my first day there by breaking things. To my relief, the man went inside and brought out a sleeping bag. I thanked him profusely and returned to my front porch, clutching that sleeping bag for dear life.

I have to say that I slept really well that night under the stars. The futon was comfortable, the sleeping bag kept me warm, the air was fresh, and Schmutz, the neighborhood cat, came over to greet me. This was the first time I had ever slept outside. Being from New York City, I had never camped or slept in a tent. Hmmm...This wasn't so bad. Perhaps I could try camping in the future.

That night ended my extreme fear of being homeless. I got to experience the energy of homelessness in as gentle a way as possible and I was free of it. Now I could move on with my life.

15

What rewards can failure bring? Freedom, joy, fun, rest, purpose!

"OK," you may ask. "I understand that you weren't happy when you were successful, but failure doesn't sound like fun either. What's so good about letting go of success? What are you getting in return?"

It's true that so far I have focused on the dismantling of my life. When you've spent over four decades building up a life based on self-betrayal, it has to be dismantled before you can build a new life based on joy. The dismantling takes time and is chaotic, but support always shows up when it's needed.

Much of my support came from my teacher, Jacob. He had established a non-profit organization dedicated to world peace through self-realization. What this means, in plain English, is that if you want to end the war out there, you need to end your internal war. Although I was still trying to find work the usual way, sending out résumés to headhunters, I began to focus on my internal process. What did I really want? What was I afraid of? How had I been betraying my self? What lies was I telling myself?

I remember a friend trying to help me get work in the corporate world. We were going over my résumé when she commented that I didn't really seem excited about finding work. The truth was that I wasn't excited at all. I didn't want to work in the business world. I wanted to work at Jacob's foundation. I wanted my skills and talents to go towards something I believed in.

Most people wait to have money so they can have the freedom to do what they want. I had always thought that money brought freedom but I realized that wasn't true for me. When I had money I had to show up at a job I didn't like twenty-four/seven. I had little vacation. Where was the freedom? But what if I didn't wait to have money? What if I decided to do what I wanted now? I wasn't working anyway; why not volunteer at the foundation?

My offer to work on the foundation's budget was gratefully accepted. The foundation was located in a town with a wonderful beach on the Pacific Ocean. I loved driving there and meeting with the director of the foundation. The staff and volunteers became close friends. It didn't feel like work at all. I was enjoying myself! Next thing I knew I was on the Board of Directors. I really wanted to be hired to work there full time but from the numbers in the budget I knew that wasn't feasible. So I looked for other ways to earn a living.

I think I mentioned that I had always wanted to be a teacher. I had already started tutoring and it was working out well. My students were doing well in school and I had earned a good reputation. Through word of mouth I started getting more and more students. It was the perfect job for me. I'm not a morning person, so I was glad that I couldn't really start tutoring until after school; 3:00 to 8:00 p.m. were perfect hours for me and sometimes I would tutor on weekends.

All of a sudden life began to flow in a way that was fun and joyful. My life was no longer compartmentalized into "work" from Monday through Friday, and "leisure" on the weekend. Work and leisure started to merge. My students and their families became friends. Some parents would have brunch for me when I tutored on Sundays or dinner if I was tutoring late. Sometimes we'd work outside by the swimming pool. Parents started confiding in me. I felt as if I were part of their families.

Since I didn't start tutoring until three o'clock, I had the whole day to do whatever I wanted. I began taking yoga on Mondays and Wednesdays in the late morning. I ran all my errands when other people were working. I did my volunteer work and sometimes I even dated. I have a fond memory of a picnic by a lake with a handsome single father who rushed to get his kids from school as I was rushing to my tutoring appointment.

I loved teaching but my income wasn't enough to support me. I needed an additional income. Lo and behold, another career began for me that I enjoyed even more than teaching.

I became a book editor.

16

Whatever your talent is, that is the work you're meant to be doing

I've had two astrological readings in my life and they both said the same thing: With four planets in Gemini, I should be writing a book or at the very least have a career in publishing. When I first heard this, I had two reactions.

The first was the gut feeling that I was hearing the truth. I have always loved writing and I write very well. When I write I seem to go into a space of "no time" where the writing writes itself. I feel peace and joy, and everything comes out perfectly edited. Often I'm surprised at the content. Events that I had forgotten find themselves on the page, bringing back all the memories and feelings associated with them.

I've always been an editor as well. When I was working in the corporate world I edited the memos written by the people who worked for me so that they would be clear and easy to understand. On occasion one of my staff would leave my office with tears in her eyes because her write-up had been totally dissected and reorganized. I sympathized but my priority was sending out a memo that was clear and readable. So I wasn't surprised that the astrologers thought I would be a good writer. I was surprised that they thought that I could actually have a career writing.

My second reaction, which came from my head, was to dismiss the idea of my being a writer as something that was airy-fairy. I had an MBA in Quantitative Analysis, for goodness sakes. I had twenty years of experience performing direct marketing analysis. That was how I made the big bucks. How on earth was I going to become a writer?

In hindsight, though, I can say that the astrologers were right on. Often we don't value our greatest talents because they are so innate that we take them for granted. We think everyone can do what we do, because it's so easy for us. Here's a secret that most people don't know: Not everyone can do what you do. Whatever your talent is, that is the work you are meant to be doing. Your life's work is meant to be joyful and creative. It's something you would do even if you didn't need the money. It's something you would look forward to doing. If you're doing work that is difficult and exhausting—if you wake up in the morning wishing you were sick so you could stay home from work—you are definitely not doing the work you came here to do.

Well, I now know that the work I am meant to do involves writing and speaking, even though I don't yet have a writing career (although if you're reading this then perhaps I do have one). Getting paid for the work isn't the priority. Do the work you love and the money will follow. Give it away for free in the beginning, to someone or some cause that you love. That's what I did.

Jacob had self-published a book he had written. The information in this book was invaluable but I thought it could be written better. I offered to edit it before it went into second printing. It was blissful sitting on my couch reading the book with a pencil in my hand, making editing changes. When I completed the editing, Jacob was very happy with the changes. The writing was smoother and clearer. That would have been payment enough for me. But that wasn't the end.

When the book was sent to the typesetter, she called me. She said that in the twenty years she had been working in the industry, she had only seen one other editor as good as I was. Did I want more work? She no longer wanted to do editing and would be happy to forward any requests for editing work to me. I was thrilled and surprised. I had no idea I was that good—and I really needed the work.

That's how my editing career started. I offered it as a gift and a great deal of high-paying work came back to me. This is another secret I have learned. Even if you have no money, even if you are afraid that you'll be homeless, you can still be generous. Instead of focusing on your lack and what you are not receiving, you can focus on giving. This shift creates the space for wonderful things to come into your life.

Editing was a lifesaver for me. It was work that I enjoyed, that paid well, that I could do at home on my own time. The fact that I could edit from home became even more important later on, when I found myself living in a small town with few employment opportunities.

But I'm jumping the gun here. That move wouldn't happen for a couple of years, when I was working for Jacob's non-profit organization.

17

Opportunities open up when you let go of your baggage

Working for Jacob was what I had wanted to do almost from the minute I met him. My heart leapt at the idea of working for his foundation, but my head said it wasn't possible. I had helped prepare the annual budget and I knew the foundation couldn't afford me. Looking back, I realize how arrogant that was. I had to downsize enough so that I could afford to work for the foundation.

It's amazing how many opportunities open up when you let go of the baggage you are carrying. Selling most of my furniture and moving to San Rafael with a housemate gave me the freedom to do only work that I loved. I loved tutoring students. I loved editing books. I was almost making ends meet when I was offered a position at the foundation. Although the salary was low, I only had to work three days a week, which would still allow me to keep all my students and continue editing. But I had to decide right away since the employee who was leaving had only given one week's notice.

This was my dream but I was also a little frightened. I asked for twenty-four hours to decide. I quickly called all my students and was easily able to change their appointments to fit into the two days I would have off. Again, everything was supporting my decision to accept the position.

The first lesson I learned from this was to not trust my

head when it tells me that something is impossible. If my heart is really excited about something, there will be a way—although not always as quickly as I would like and not necessarily in the way I expect.

The second lesson was that when opportunity knocks, you have to go for it. There isn't much time to debate and plan. Just follow your heart and take a leap of faith. So I began to work for my teacher's foundation.

The third lesson was that, even if you're following your heart and doing your life's work, challenges will come up. My first couple of months at the foundation were both heaven and hell.

I was warmly welcomed by the staff, who were like family to me. The small office space was just a five-minute walk from the ocean, which I loved. As a customer service rep—that was my new job—I got to have heartfelt conversations with people who had seen Jacob on TV and were on fire for truth and freedom. But—there is always a but—the work had a steep learning curve and I had a great deal to learn. The employee I was replacing didn't have much time to train me. The director of the foundation and I often clashed. I had an hour commute each way. I wound up putting in twelve-hour days. How funny that even working for a spiritual foundation in this small town, I could create the stressful work environment that I had in New York.

The fourth lesson I learned is that it's much easier to be spiritual when you're on retreat than when you are at work—but it is possible to be spiritual even when you have more work than you can handle. Even though I felt very stressed about all the work, I had not really recreated my jobs in New York and in San Francisco. The staff at the foundation actually walked their talk. Being loving and telling the truth was not something that was reserved for the retreats—it was practiced in the work environment. Issues came up but they were addressed in a very conscious way. They weren't suppressed and they weren't acted out. It was a different way of being that took some getting used to. I felt as if I had come back home from a long war, and hadn't yet figured out that the war was over.

But the war did seem to be over. Yes, there was work to be done and long commutes and staff meetings and budgets. But there was also respect and love and compassion and truth.

And there were wonderful retreats...

18

A retreat creates the space to meet yourself

In the four-year period during which I was involved with the foundation, I had more retreats than God. Some were one-day retreats while others lasted two weeks. Some were in locations specifically set up for retreats, such as Esalen; others were in cosmopolitan areas such as New York and Los Angeles; others were in historical villages in Europe such as Assisi, Italy; and many were in my home town. What they all had in common was that they carved out a space for me to uncover who I truly am underneath all the neuroses and conditioned responses.

I highly recommend taking some time off—even a weekend or a day—to devote to something that will nourish your soul. A vacation that includes a lot of sightseeing, socializing, or sports doesn't count. What counts is stopping the usual activities and having the intent to discover at a deeper level what you really want.

I have a friend who is married and has four children and three dogs. Every now and then she takes time off by herself, goes to the seaside, reads a good book, lights some candles, plays music she likes, and enjoys the quiet. Once a year she attends a week-long retreat for women only, in Sea Ranch on the California coast.

Whenever I'd prepare to go on a retreat, I thought of it as a vacation. I looked forward to the beautiful location where it would be held, to the delicious food that would be served, to reuniting with my friends, and to soaking in the wisdom that would be offered. I looked forward to the love I felt for everyone when I was in that sacred space. I looked forward to the joy and the playfulness as well. And I did receive all of the above.

However, I received much more than that—and I can't say that it was all comfortable. When the discomfort arose, that's when I'd remember a retreat is so much more than a vacation. Because my commitment was to waking up—which meant waking up to the unconscious behavioral patterns that caused my suffering—I usually got to see these patterns in living color. I got to see how my arrogance separates me from the people I love and how it hurts them. I got to see how I try to control situations and people so that I will feel safe. I got to see the fears I've been keeping at bay by being busy.

Being busy may deflect the fears for a while but they are always just below the surface, waiting to be met. More than just allowing the space to relax and renew, a retreat creates the space to meet your *self* at a deeper level—both the dark side and the light side. A retreat can help you get in touch with what you really want.

19

What do you really want?

What do you really want? That's the question that has been asked at the retreats I attended, and it really is the most important question you can ask yourself. Until you answer it, all your actions are meaningless. It's like trying to plan a trip when you don't know your destination. Why bother?

Most of us have a long list of desires. I know that I did. In decreasing order of importance, they were:

- to be successful at a high-paying job;

- to have a soul mate/life partner;

- to look beautiful;

- to own a beautiful home with nice furniture;

- to own a sexy, elegant wardrobe;

- to be respected and admired.

Well, the list went on and on, but really the two first desires were the main ones.

I needed the successful high-paying job so I would be respected and admired, and so that I could afford the beautiful home, the nice furniture, the elegant wardrobe, and all the beauty treatments (hair cut, hair color, pedicure, manicure, waxing, etc.).

Looking beautiful was important so that I could attract a man—*The One*—whom I would marry and with whom I would live happily ever after. I didn't want a man to take care of me nor did I want to start a family. The longing for a man was at a much deeper, spiritual level. I wanted a union at all levels: physical (great sex was really important), emotional, intellectual (interesting discussions were also important), and spiritual. This union would make me whole and bring me happiness.

Well, the good news was that I got the high-paying job and realized that it didn't make me happy. The bad news was that no matter how hard I tried and no matter how good I looked, I couldn't find *The One*. Oh, there were plenty of men who were attracted to me, but all those relationships ended in suffering. None of the men were capable of true intimacy (in hindsight I realize that I wasn't capable of true intimacy either), and I found myself clinging and manipulating, trying to get their attention. The more I tried, the more distant they became, until it was more painful being in relationship with them than being alone. Finally I would end the relationship to put us both out of our misery.

When I met Jacob and he asked the question "*What do you want? If you could only have one desire, if it was with your dying breath, what would it be*?" I realized that my longing had been misplaced. I wasn't longing for a man. I was longing to be Home. I was longing to find myself. I was longing for true love—not the syrupy romantic kind where you pretend to be someone you are not so that you can be loved—but the kind of true love that tells the truth ruthlessly and allows you to be who you really are.

If I had only one desire, with my dying breath, that desire was for Freedom. I wanted to be released from the prison I had created out of everything I had been taught and all the expectations I believed everyone else had of me. I was tired of being the "good girl" so that I would be liked. I was tired of being the employee who was willing to give her all for the job so that I could earn the big bucks. I was tired of looking sexy all the time so that I could attract some man. I was plain tired.

Yes, I wanted to be Home, so that I could rest. And then I remembered all the recurring dreams I had about trying to find my way Home.

20

Recurring dreams have a message

I believe that dreams serve many functions. Some dreams help heal subconscious layers of the psyche or, at the very least, they deliver a message to let you know where you are stuck. If you're experiencing a recurring dream, pay attention. It is probably trying to send you an important message.

When I was married to Michael and living the successful life, the recurring dream I had was of vampires. I was in my house, the sun was setting, and I knew there were vampires outside. Once the sun set, these vampires would show up. My only hope was to find a cross that I had been given years ago. Desperately I searched through my jewelry box looking for the cross but I couldn't find it. All of a sudden it was night and I could see the vampire faces at the window.

At that point, I always woke up in a cold sweat. I couldn't understand the meaning of the dream. Later, I figured it out. The dreams were telling me that I had really ventured far from Home, that I was in danger, and that I was desperately looking for the spirituality I had lost so that I could be saved.

Thank God these nightmares disappeared after my divorce when I started finding myself again. They were replaced by a recurring dream that wasn't quite as fearful, though it was anxiety provoking. In this dream I have tickets for a flight Home (sometimes it's on a ship). The tickets are for the same day and I know I have plenty of time to make the flight if I leave right away. The problem is that I haven't packed anything and I am desperately trying to pack a suitcase. I don't want to leave my stuff behind but I am afraid that I will miss the flight if I pack everything. I arrive at the airport and I am running for dear life to catch the flight Home.

At this point, I usually woke up with my heart beating fast. Again, at the time I didn't understand what the meaning of the dream was. Later, I figured it out. It was pretty obvious. I was longing to be Home but clinging to all my material possessions was creating an obstacle. I needed to let go of my attachment to my stuff so that I would be free to find my way.

Years later, after I met Jacob and had downsized quite a bit, I had a couple of updated versions of the dream. In one dream I finally made it on the plane and it took off. In another dream I was on a boat that had arrived Home but the boat was too big to dock at the harbor. Small boats were arriving to take us to the shore. I could see Home at a distance; it sort of looked like New York. The woman who was driving my small boat arrived to pick me up. I asked her if she could wait an hour so that I could pack but she said no. I was very annoyed. Even though I had downsized, I still wanted to take the few things that I had with me. But finally I had to give the stuff up.

The most recent "coming Home" dream indicated that I was already Home. There was nothing to do, no place to go. All I needed to do was to realize that I was already Home.

Part 2

Breaking Free from the Spiritual Trance

1. The pursuit of enlightenment
    replaces the pursuit of success

2. Spiritual community or cult?

3. The honeymoon period lasts six months

4. A different kind of judgment

5. The medicine becomes a poison

6. Sacrificing for a cause?

7. Freedom from suffering?

8. What's so spiritual about being poor?

9. What is there to be afraid of?

10. Meeting life replaces meeting death

11. A way of life ends

12. My prayer is answered

13. The guru falls

14. The victim/hero/villain triangle

15. Manifesting a happy life

1

The pursuit of enlightenment replaces the pursuit of success

I wish I had really understood the meaning of that dream telling me that I was already Home. Alas, I pursued enlightenment with the same vigor with which I had previously pursued money.

When I first met Jacob, I remember telling him that I wished he had an ashram. I would have been happy to shave my head, wear white clothes (or whatever color clothes nuns wear), and eat gruel. He laughed and said it wasn't about that. But somehow it seemed I had taken vows of poverty and chastity.

The chastity thing happened on its own. The man I was dating disappeared and I wasn't interested in meeting anyone else. The poverty thing was partially my choice. I chose to work for Jacob's foundation despite the fact that it didn't pay very well and there were never any raises.

Still, I was happy. I felt I was of service. I got to attend retreats for free, sit in front of Jacob, and bask in the light of his wisdom. I met a community of people whom I loved. I was feeling more love than I had ever felt before. All that was good.

What wasn't good were the spiritual concepts that I imposed on myself. Rules on how to be successful were replaced with rules on how to be spiritual:

- Instead of being arrogant and confident, I needed to be humble.

- Instead of being a fast paced multi-tasker, I needed to slow down and become silent.

- Instead of being aggressive and acting like a man to succeed, I needed to embrace the feminine qualities of receptivity and compassion.

- Instead of trying to fill my life up with stuff, I needed to empty it out.

- Instead of seeking more money, I needed to accept poverty as it showed me what was really important—love.

The list went on and on. Some of the concepts were so subtle that it took me years to figure out they were there. But while my mind couldn't figure out what was wrong, my body and heart knew. Perhaps I wasn't as happy as I thought. My stomach felt tight. I was concerned that people would think that I wasn't awake. I found myself trying to imitate what I considered to be enlightened behavior. People walked around smiling, hugging each other, staring into each other's eyes, and I found myself imitating them. I couldn't do it for long, though, because I found that a nauseous feeling would come over me.

I later learned that I could really trust that feeling of nausea. It meant that something wasn't true; it wasn't real; it was a poor, syrupy imitation of the real thing. This feeling really became an important guide for me, especially after we all moved to a place that I will call Shangri-La, to become a spiritual community.

2

Spiritual community or cult?

At one of our retreats Jacob had asked us to examine "commitment, community, and cult." Our reading assignment was *Enlightenment Blues,* a book written about a spiritual teacher, Andrew Cohen, that discussed the horrors of a spiritual community that had become a cult. I was so grateful that I had a spiritual teacher who was above all that, and I took an oath that I would never allow our community to become a cult—not if it were in my power.

My oath would be put to the test when we moved to Shangri-La. Jacob and his wife, Lakshmi, who was also a well known spiritual teacher with her own foundation, went to Shangri-La in the summer of 2004 to host a retreat. They really enjoyed the town and were invited by the spiritual community to move there. They found the invitation interesting and sent the staff of both foundations an e-mail, inviting us to their home to discuss the possibility of moving north from Marin.

The instant I read the e-mail I knew we were going to move. I had never been to Shangri-La but had heard it was a beautiful town surrounded by mountains, with four distinct seasons, some good restaurants, and even theater. Hmmmm... It had been a long time since I had been to the theater. I realized I missed some of the culture I had left behind in New York.

When Jacob and Lakshmi returned home, we all

gathered at their house to discuss the move. Jacob was excited and had wonderful things to say about the town. The only negative was that you couldn't find good dim-sum (he was right about that). Shangri-La was a large college town and I could find students to tutor there, he told me. His excitement started to rub off on everyone.

One by one, he asked each person to discuss his or her feelings about the move. Everyone was honest. Most people wanted to move. It seemed we were all losing our ties to Marin. In my case, a one-year relationship with a man whom I loved had just ended; he would have been my only tie to Marin. There was only one woman on staff who tearfully admitted she could not move. She had just been married and had bought a house in the Bay Area.

Since several of us had never been to Shangri-La, we were invited to take some time off from work and, at the foundation's expense, visit the town to make a final decision. A couple of weeks later eight of us caravanned to visit what would be our new home. I had fun. I loved the people I worked with but didn't usually get time to spend with them outside of work and the retreats. The Bay Area is large and most of us lived scattered in differ-ent areas—Marin, Berkeley, Sonoma, the South Bay. I enjoyed hanging out with my coworkers and dreamed of living in close proximity as a community.

I have to admit there was one point during the trip when I freaked out. I was sitting in the hot tub when it occurred to me how small Shangri-La was—only about twenty thousand inhabitants—with no large cities near-by. I imagined not having any privacy, being surrounded constantly by the same people, not being able to escape. I was having a hard time breathing but I quickly got over this anxiety attack and decided I would move to Shangri-La.

So did everyone else, with the exception of the woman who had just been married. The next couple of months were exciting. We found the perfect office building in Shangri-La to house both foundations. The only problem was that it was next to a McDonald's. Our bodies were temples and not only would we never eat at a McDonald's, we had a hard time working next to one. However, God was on our side and the McDonald's closed before we moved. That was a good sign!

About twenty of us were moving at the foundation's expense, and we were all looking for housing. Other followers wanted to move as well, but they were told to wait. We didn't want to disturb the small community of Shangri-La and it wasn't necessary for people who weren't on staff to move. All good.

In November of 2004 I packed my two cats, Max and Bradley, and drove north to our new home. I had found what I thought was the perfect little cottage in the historic district. It was owned by a man in our spiritual group, Frank, and his wife, Lara. When I arrived exhausted from the packing, the driving, and the cats howling, Lara was there to greet us and to help us get settled. I felt I had arrived home.

I thought that the rest of my life was planned. I would work for Jacob's foundation surrounded by my co-workers and friends, who were all very spiritual, live in Shangri-La in a cute cottage with my cats, and eventually become enlightened. Ha! Little did I know...

3

The honeymoon period lasts six months

My honeymoon with Shangri-La lasted six months.

There were many wonderful things about Shangri-La. For one, there was no traffic—ever. Not only was the office just a five-minute drive from my house but everything in Shangri-La was just a five-minute drive from my house. Good-bye long commutes and sitting in a car for hours. I never did like driving ...

In addition, our office was located across the street from a fantastic bakery. Each morning I had coffee and a morning muffin and each afternoon I took a break to have chocolate mousse. Yum! The fact that it was cold out and got dark really early added to my desire for comfort food.

The first Friday of every month, the town had an Art Walk. The art galleries (yes, it's a sophisticated little town) would all stay open until eight o'clock—serving wine, cheese, and desserts—and you could walk from one gallery to another, running into all the people you knew.

The spiritual community that was already living in Shangri-La embraced us, inviting us to potluck dinners and holiday celebrations. In addition we got to hang out with each other—a lot. One of my best friends, Trudy, moved up to Shangri-La as well and rented a cottage down the lane from mine. In addition to being a good friend she is a great cook and would often invite me to dinner.

Lara, my landlady, also invited me to dinner. Whenever I needed help, she was there to help me hang up paintings, take boxes to the dump—she even created a little cat window so that Max and Bradley could go in and out of the cottage easily. I felt very safe and secure in this idyllic environment, but I would soon find out there is no true security.

4

A different kind of judgment

Did I mention that Shangri-La was a small town? And that the people I worked with—not to mention Jacob and Lakshmi—all lived within five minutes of each other? And that the spiritual community was dedicated to awakening—that is to becoming self-realized and dropping the ego?

Well, people weren't judged in Shangri-la by how rich they were. Most people, including me and the other employees of the foundation, had very little money. Certainly material success was not considered a measure of worth—and that's a good thing. It would have been great if people had not been judged on any basis but, unfortunately, that was not the case. People were judged—they were judged on the basis of how "awake" they were.

One of the members of our community was angry with Jacob because he told her, at one of the retreats, that she was not awake. A new hierarchy was being born, one based on how close you were to the teacher, or how awake you were considered to be. In reaction I found myself saying that I was not awake and I didn't care about awakening. This need to be awake was becoming a tight girdle and I didn't feel like I could breathe in it. I soon received a phone call from a friend who worked with me—and was also a therapist—who had heard me state that I didn't care about being awake. He offered me a free therapy session to support my realization that I was awake. Who had asked him? I was offended and I told him so.

Awake, awake, awake. It was becoming a mantra. My friend Trudy used to joke by asking, "Who is giving out the awake pins?" Who, indeed? Well, Jacob for one.

Rachel was one of the women who worked closely with Jacob. She traveled with him, she cooked for him, and she took care of him. I had run into them a few times at the grocery store and was surprised to see how comfortable she was with him. Whenever I ran into Jacob I would get flustered and be concerned that I didn't sound "awake" enough. Not Rachel. She was never flustered and I was told that she was *awake*. She was self-realized. Hmmmm... She didn't seem awake to me. But Jacob was asking her to hold *satsang*—a public meeting where an enlightened teacher sits with students in meditation, offering an enlightened transmission and answering spiritual questions.

I didn't really know her very well as she wasn't the friendliest of women. She wasn't a very good "organization" person either, but Jacob kept trying to find work for her at the foundation. When we first moved to Shangri-La I wound up having lunch with her to discuss some work issues. Starting with some casual chitchat, she asked me if I thought I would have a partner some day. Yes, I did see myself with a partner at some point. How about her? "Oh, no," she replied, "those days are over for me."

I was surprised. She was a young, attractive woman but she wasn't interested in men. Well, she had a daughter and had been through a rough time. Maybe her pursuits were of a higher nature. Maybe she really was awake and I just didn't understand her.

My confusion around Rachel would be put aside as I was, once again, dealt a blow that ended my illusion of security.

71

5

The medicine becomes a poison

Enough already. I understood that the spiritual path involved loss and having your worst fears show up but was there no end to this? Of course my fears involve money, so once again I found myself out on a limb.

When we moved to Shangri-La, I had much less work to do at the foundation. In the beginning this was a relief but soon I became bored. The pastry shop beckoned more and more and by the time the winter was over I had gained over ten pounds and couldn't fit into my spring clothes. This was the least of my worries. When I asked to meet with the director of the foundation to ask her for more work, she informed me that they had to let me go.

I was shocked. They had moved me to Shangri-La six months before and now I was being laid off in a town that had no work—not above minimum wage, anyway. What was I going to do? I could tell that the director was heartbroken. She was crying and that made me feel a little bit better—at least she cared—but how was I going to earn a living? I was given a month's severance and I was eligible for unemployment, so I had some time. It was a Friday. I went home and spent the weekend in bed, shaking from fear.

I understood that laying me off was a financial decision; it wasn't personal. I tried to be strong. I told everyone I was fine and I even continued to do some volunteer work for the foundation for a while. But I wasn't fine. Besides being terrified about how I was going to pay the rent, I was also hurt. I was hurt that Jacob never mentioned anything to me nor did he say he was sorry that he had to let me go. I was hurt that Lakshmi lightly said to me that I knew how to make money and I would be fine. I didn't know if I would be fine. And I wasn't. For a year and a half I tried to make ends meet and I couldn't. The advice from friends in the community was that this was an opportunity for me to meet my fears. In doing so I would awaken.

This "meeting death" thing was becoming old. The medicine that Jacob had once offered—the advice to meet your fear and not run away from it—had now become a poison. Rather than supporting me, it was adding to my suffering. It wasn't bad enough that I was feeling terrible every month as I tried to figure out how to pay the rent. I was adding to my suffering by feeling that I had failed in meeting the terror and awakening.

Desperately I looked for work in a town that is meant for retired people, tourists, and spiritual gurus. The tutoring that Jacob promised I would find wasn't going to support me. While I could earn a hundred dollars an hour tutoring in the Bay Area, I would be lucky if I could earn ten dollars an hour tutoring in Shangri-La. I considered teaching math at the university but I would barely get minimum wage there as well. I tried editing books long distance but just couldn't get enough work. I even tried working for another spiritual teacher and his partner, but after three weeks I resigned in order to maintain my sanity. In accepting this short-lived job, I lost the unemployment I was receiving.

What I wonder now, in hindsight, is why no one gave

me the only advice that would have made sense: *Move! Leave Shangri-La! If you can't find work here, go somewhere where you can find work. Go back to the Bay Area.*

I have found that people pursuing enlightenment can get so involved in complicated spiritual concepts that they lose sight of practical solutions and common sense. Ugh! But I wasn't the only one suffering…

6

Sacrificing for a cause?

It seemed that many people who had moved to Shangri-La to be with Jacob and the spiritual community were suffering—mostly financially. A couple of friends who had moved from Berkeley were contemplating bankruptcy. The husband was a contractor who couldn't find work in Shangri-La. Well, he was actually working on Jacob's second house, but he was being paid much less than the hourly rate he had earned in the Bay Area.

Jacob and Lakshmi were not suffering financially. They bought a beautiful home in Shangri-La, by a creek, and when the neighboring house was up for sale, the foundation bought it for them as well. They could host small group meetings there. My friend wasn't the only one working on this house. During a retreat in Shangri-La, on their day off, a hundred attendees volunteered for a day of service, working at this house. I was no longer involved with the foundation and something did not sit right with me when I heard from some of the devotees—for that is what they had become—what a joyful experience it was to clear out rocks and do manual labor for this house.

Actually, at this point many things weren't sitting well with me. I had always had issues with financial aspects of the foundation, since the very first day that I started working on the budget. I was surprised to find that when

Jacob and Lakshmi taught in New York, they stayed in a suite at the Trump Tower. There was no way a New York retreat could be profitable, given their expenses.

Actually, the only retreats that were very profitable were the ones that were held wherever Jacob was living, since he was not spending tens of thousands of dollars on hotels, restaurants, and other expenses. When I commented on the extravagance, the director of the foundation told me our job was to make sure Jacob was comfortable. Nothing else mattered.

I had no idea how much effort went to keeping him comfortable, but I soon found out. During a retreat in New York, the director asked me if I would take her place because she wasn't going to go. The foundation would pay my airfare to New York, which was a godsend as I had no money. Since I thought I was being asked to handle the business end—make announcements at the retreats, etc.—I happily accepted. Had I known that my job was to take care of Jacob and Lakshmi's personal needs, I would have reconsidered.

I knew I was in trouble when I was presented with a twenty-page dossier describing everything that needed to be done to take care of them. It included several lists of necessary groceries and the stores from which to buy them. Every morning I was supposed to go to a particular deli and get a specific kind of fresh-squeezed juice, place it in a bag that I had been given to keep it cold, bring it to the hotel, and leave it outside their door.

Their luggage arrived at the Trump Tower before they did. I needed to unpack so everything was in its place when they got there. Thank God that a friend, Hannah, who lived on the Upper West Side—the perfect Jewish mother—was also assigned the task of taking care of Jacob. For the most part I felt helpless, as nurturing others and doing housework are not skills I possess. She carried most of the load as we unpacked the special tea-pot and the special bowls that traveled with them, and the cosmetics that were to go into their separate bath-rooms.

The trickiest part was that after New York we were all going upstate to the Omega Institute for another retreat. Hannah and I needed to wait until Jacob and Lakshmi checked out of the Trump, then pack everything up and arrive upstate and unpack it all again—and we needed to do this before they arrived. I actually don't remem-ber how we accomplished this feat. What I do remember was the stress of being at our leaders' beck and call. And I wasn't even doing the work! Hannah drove them back and forth to their meetings and brought them their food in plastic containers since they did not eat in the dining room with the rest of us.

I won't go on, but you get the idea. What didn't sit well with me was that the foundation barely paid its em-ployees a living wage. For example, the man who did the videotaping often drove the van cross-country to reach the retreats, but he had to supplement his income from his savings. At least he was getting paid. Others who worked at the office were unpaid volunteers. I was one of the lucky few.

Working for free was expected. That's what devotees did. We were of service. Money was nothing compared to what was being offered: awakening and freedom from suffering.

7

Freedom from suffering?

Freedom from suffering? That wasn't my experience. The suffering I had experienced in New York was replaced with a different kind of suffering.

In New York I had plenty of money but I was stressed at work, felt empty, and had few friends and no community to speak of. In Shangri-La I had plenty of friends, a supportive community, and I felt alive spiritually, but I had no money.

It was a miracle that the rent got paid each month. Actually, I started renting out a room in my house to people who were visiting Shangri-La and attending retreats. That helped some. Still, there were times when I didn't have money to buy groceries and I had to eat peanut butter and crackers every night for dinner. There were times when I would go to the grocery store just to eat some of the samples they were offering. I lived in constant fear of being hungry or being homeless.

I hadn't bought clothes in years. I lived in yoga pants and clogs in the winter, and cotton dresses in the summer. Actually, I exaggerate a bit here. I did buy a few dresses while I was in Shangri-La. There was a consignment shop called Déjà Vu that sold some really pretty things. I found dresses for six dollars each and bought four of them. I felt rich. I have to admit that I still wear these dresses and receive compliments when I do. But shopping was not what I worried about, nor did I miss it.

What was really difficult for me was not being able to pay my bills. I'm one of those people who likes to pay her bills early. I get pleasure out of having everything in order. At the end of every month, as the time approached to pay the rent, I would go into a deep terror. My new landlord was a nice man who took great care of the house. The idea of not fulfilling my part of the agreement stressed me out more than anything else in my life.

At one point I started losing my hair. I actually had two very large bald spots on the left side, where I part my hair. I had been so very proud of my hair up to that point. It was thick, dark, and shiny, and I always received compliments on it. All of a sudden it was falling out in handfuls. I could see the skin on my scalp. I had to start parting in on the right side to hide my bald spots and I was horrified at the prospect there might come a time when I couldn't hide my baldness anymore.

It was ironic that just the month before, my hairdresser had commented that I had such thick hair I would never have to worry about losing it. Ha! I guess this was just another attachment that I needed to face—the attachment to my hair, the attachment to being young and beautiful. I had been told by my teacher that the path to awakening was a path of loss. I hadn't realized the path included hair loss.

In the beginning I thought my hair loss was due to menopause. I had read that this happened. But when I went to my hairdresser to have my long hair cut off— there was no point in keeping it very long since it just created more of a mess on the floor when it fell—she told me that she had seen this happen before. My hair loss was stress related. She assured me that my hair would grow back, but it would probably be white. I didn't care if it grew back green. I was coloring my hair anyway. Just please, God, let it grow back.

Wasn't being poor enough?

8

What's so spiritual about being poor?

As I mentioned, I wasn't the only one suffering financially. Most of my spiritual community had money issues, and so did the larger Shangri-La community.

It's hard to explain what it's like living in this town. There is a loving, peaceful energy in Shangri-La. The people are kind and supportive—at least the ones I met. Most of them are on some kind of spiritual path. The entire town feels like a spiritual vortex. It makes sense that many spiritual teachers live there and that many retreats are offered in this town. People come to Shangri-La, enjoy the beauty, attend retreats, do some processing, and go home. Shangri-La is a great place to visit.

Those visitors not on a spiritual path, with money, can enjoy the theater, restaurants, shopping. There! I said it. This is the crux of the problem. The world seemed to be divided into two groups: those who had money and weren't spiritual, and those who were spiritual and didn't have money. Of course this is just another spiritual trance but it seemed to be pervasive in Shangri-La. The spiritual community seems to be cloaked with a scarcity belief that is numbing. Many people earn only nine dollars an hour. An hourly wage of fifteen dollars is considered really good.

While the town is peaceful, it lacks a sense of aliveness. It's the opposite of the frenetic New York energy that is so stressful, but from my perspective it's still not ideal. What is ideal to me is an energy that is somewhere in the middle—grounded and alive. I experience it living now in the San Francisco Bay Area. The aliveness that comes from creativity and abundance is missing in Shangri-La.

The two years I spent living in Shangri-La involved mostly psychological and spiritual processing—meeting my fears, seeing my attachments, etc. Nothing much happened externally there. Certainly I wasn't productive which didn't bother me, although I was stressed about not being able to fulfill my financial obligations. A strong belief in productivity is part of the material trance to which I no longer subscribe. But there is such a thing as showing up in the world—contributing and having abundance—rather than escaping it.

Living in Shangri-La—actually the entire five years that I pursued enlightenment with a passion—was like having my car in a garage for major repairs. All the work was done on myself, internally. But finally there comes a time when the car is repaired and it's time to take it on the road. That's what the car is about—traveling. Sitting in silence and sharing the same spiritual truths over and over can become old, unless you are in fact an enlightened saint.

I once wrote to Jacob telling him that our spiritual community in Shangri-La had become the cult of the "silent, staring, smiling" people. In meetings I found myself speaking—often discussing something that was bothering me—only to find everyone staring back at me, smiling beatifically. But no one responded. They had been taught to be "true friends."

Being a true friend meant that you listened to someone without judging, without agreeing, without trying to fix them. You were simply present to them, listening. Again, this was wonderful medicine when Jacob first taught us to show up this way. People rarely truly listen because they are too busy thinking about how they will respond. Unfortunately in Shangri-La it became a poison. I wondered if anyone was there. I wondered what they thought. I longed for someone to say something—anything—to me. I longed for a spontaneous response.

To Jacob's credit, he is not a silent, staring, smiling clone. Yes, he does smile a lot. That's what attracted me to him in the first place. And there is a quiet in his presence that you can rest in—that is the silence that he talks about. But outwardly he is a boisterous New Yorker, full of life, a sense of humor, and, yes, even anger. It's sad that people pick up and imitate certain aspects of their teachers without going inside and sharing what is truly coming up for them.

But then again, some of these students are just afraid.

9

What is there to be afraid of?

I found that most people in meetings with Jacob were afraid to say anything negative. They were afraid to express their fears, and they were certainly afraid to express anger. Many people raised their hands to express how grateful they were to Jacob, or how loving they were, or how blissful they were. Sometimes I heard them and really felt their transmission. I knew they were telling the truth. Most of the time, however, I got that nauseous feeling that told me they were faking it.

I, on the other hand, usually spoke out when I had some issue coming up and needed help. This meant I was usually feeling upset, angry, or frightened when I spoke to Jacob. It's not that I didn't feel grateful, loving, or blissful at times. But when I felt that way I tended to sit back and appreciate the moment. I didn't need the whole world to know.

Many people who heard me speak in anger or address difficult issues were surprised. They would come to me afterwards and tell me how they admired that I could speak up. Again, to Jacob's credit, he didn't seem to have a problem with me when I did this. He usually addressed my issue in a matter-of-fact way, without taking anything personally. I loved that about him and that showed me he was a true teacher.

But he was changing in Shangri-La. He seemed to

get denser. He seemed more removed. Some shift was happening that I didn't understand. As I mentioned, I felt that the community was becoming cultish—not because of anything he was doing but because of the trips that we were laying on each other as a spiritual community. I had a sense he didn't know what was going on as he was, in fact, removed from the community. Since I was no longer working for the foundation, people expressed fears to me that they would not express to others.

The last retreat I attended with Jacob was a silent retreat in April, 2006. It was offered for free, which meant that I could afford it. In the midst of all the beatific discussions, I stood up to say that I was concerned that our spiritual community was becoming a cult. "Why hasn't anyone told me?" Jacob challenged me.

"Well, everyone is afraid of you!" I replied.

The truth is Jacob could be very tough. He had a no-nonsense way of dealing with people that could be intense. He could be sarcastic. He definitely could offend people. One of his favorite remarks in describing Christianity was that it was "the cult of the dead Jew on a stick." Fortunately, I had rarely experienced that side of him. But on this day, he was tough. He told me I used to be an uptight bitch but was no longer uptight.

Something shifted for me on that day. Up until that point I felt that all his comments—even the tough or insulting ones—were for my own good. I saw myself as a spiritual warrior for Truth, not afraid to stand up and take blows for the grander purpose of Awakening. But at this retreat I found myself leaving the room in tears. Friends came to console me despite the fact that it was breaking confidentiality (we weren't supposed to discuss anything that occurred in the retreat afterwards).

At the end of the retreat Jacob sat on a chair while

people came to pay their respects and say good-bye. This was unusual for him. I didn't remember him doing that before. It seemed to me like he was in fact becoming a guru—even though he had often said he was not that.

I had no interest in saying good-bye to him but unfortunately I ran into him as I was leaving the hall. His cold stare told me I was done. I had found a teacher who was very much like me: an outspoken New Yorker, smart, with a sense of humor and a sarcastic wit, who could easily belittle people. Hmmmm... Where was kindness and compassion in all of this?

I prayed that if there were a kind, compassionate teacher out there, I wanted to meet him or her. Until then, I was done with teachers. I soon heard about Ammachi.

10

Meeting life replaces meeting death

When I hear about something three times, I take notice. It's usually something I need to know or someone I need to meet. The week after my prayer for a compassionate, kind teacher, three different people mentioned Ammachi to me. I had never heard of her. She is an Indian saint known as the "hugging saint" because she goes around the world hugging people. Thousands of people line up to get hugged by her, as her hugs are life changing. Through her hugs she is able to transmit a spiritual energy that has a tremendous affect on people. Not only that, she is involved in many charity projects and has donated millions of dollars to help tsunami victims.

When my friend Trudy told me she was driving from Shangri-La to the Bay Area to see Ammachi, I jumped at the chance to go with her. As happens when I'm supposed to do something, everything fell into place. Trudy's client was paying for the gas, so I didn't need to contribute any money. That was good, since I didn't have any money. A friend in the Bay Area was away and offered us her lovely apartment for the trip. So off we went to get hugged by Ammachi.

When we walked into the ashram I was struck by how different spiritual paths can be. With Jacob, meetings were quiet. People sat in silence waiting for him to come in. Rarely were there any children in the room. Emptiness seemed to be the main flavor at Jacob's retreats. The experience at Ammachi's ashram was one of fullness.

All my senses were overwhelmed at Ammachi's. There were beautiful colored flowers—mostly lotuses and roses. Their scent and the scent of perfumed essential oils permeated the huge room. People were chanting as they awaited Ammachi's entrance. Upstairs you could have a massage or a Vedic astrology session. Older kids were running around playing while mothers held babies in their arms. There was a cafeteria with great food and the best chai that I have tasted. And there was shopping. Yes, while this saint was up on stage hugging people, you could actually buy jewelry, clothing, perfumes, books, statues of Hindu gods and goddesses, or sheets that Ammachi had slept in. Wow! It was like being at a spiritual carnival.

Not that I was tempted to become a Hindu or a follower of another teacher, even if she was a saint. I could see how some of her followers wore the right clothes but were controlling and had issues. I could see that following any teacher would have its traps. The only teacher I would follow from now on was my own heart.

What I appreciated about the ashram was that it showed me another way to awaken. Besides meeting death, you could meet life, and I realized that both were necessary. After being mesmerized by the material world I needed to wake up and see that there was an entire internal world waiting to be explored. But after focusing on the internal world for years, the external world was beckoning again.

Ammachi walked in and I was lucky enough to be up front. She reminded me of a mountain. She walked past people, offering up her hands so that people could touch them, and made it to the stage. We had been given tokens so we would know when it was time to go up and get hugged. Since this was our first time, we got to be among the first to go up. This was great, as sometimes people wait for ten hours or more to get hugged. Ammachi can sit on the stage from six p.m. until noon the next day, hugging people without having food, or water, or a bathroom break. She's not quite human. She seems to get her energy directly from the Source. I did get to see the difference between someone who is a saint, and someone who is awake. (I aspire to be the latter.)

The hug probably took less than ten seconds but when I got up I felt drunk. People had to help me stay steady on my feet and for the next few hours I was a bit out of it. I was surprised by the intensity of the energy. What I didn't know was how my life would change.

11

A way of life ends

A few days later Trudy and I returned home and I knew that my days in Shangri-La were numbered. As I sat in the front yard of my home, I remember being taken over by a huge fear that felt like death. I knew my life in Shangri-La was ending but I had no idea where to go or what to do.

As I sat there shaking, I noticed my landlord had planted strawberries that were bearing fruit. I stopped and tasted one and it was delicious. I recalled a story about a man who was being chased by a tiger. To escape he jumped off the cliff and was caught by a branch on a tree. The branch wasn't going to hold him and there was another tiger waiting for him below. But he saw a strawberry, picked it, and had the most delicious strawberry that he had ever tasted. This was a lesson in being in the moment. That story flashed into my mind as I tasted the strawberry. Oh-oh. I was going to be in trouble.

Well, it wasn't a surprise when the time finally came that I had to move out of my house. There was no way I was going to come up with the rent money. It was a month after my hug, the end of July, and I had to face the hard truth. I could not live in this house and I could not live in Shangri-La anymore. I gave a month's notice, which was covered by the deposit I had given when I first moved. I had until the end of September to find a new home. Where would I go?

I started looking for work in the San Francisco Bay Area. Direct marketing jobs were available and I was hoping I might have an offer before I moved. One job at an ad agency in Mill Valley seemed particularly promising and I was devastated when I didn't get it. That was my last hope.

The month of September went by quickly. At this point I didn't mind leaving Shangri-La. The summer in Shangri-La had been very hot and my house didn't have air conditioning. One week in particular, the temperature had been over a hundred degrees every day. I felt as if I were in hell. I flashed back to the time when I decided to leave New York after a hot summer where I was miserable and contemplating death. I guess this was my pattern. The universe created an intolerably hot environment that made me want to move from a place I had loved.

I no longer had any emotional ties to Jacob or the spiritual community around him. When I returned from my trip to Ammachi I received an e-mail from Jacob. The subject line said, "Love." The first line of the e-mail said, "Dear Despina, I am sorry to hear…" My heart opened. Jacob did care! He had heard I was leaving Shangri-La because I had no money and he was writing to tell me that he was sorry. That's what I thought.

Wrong. As I read on, the e-mail said, "I am sorry to hear that you have made me the cause of your suffering." He then went on to say he had heard I was angry with him. The e-mail ended with, "When gratitude is lost, hell becomes your home."

I was shocked. First of all, I wasn't angry with him. Second, I couldn't believe that he had used the title "Love." Third, I couldn't imagine who he had heard from.

I thought and thought. Then I remembered that I had shared with my friend Trudy, weeks ago, that I had been angry with Jacob for moving me to Shangri-La and dumping me there but that I had processed through that. She must have shared that with her boyfriend who worked for Jacob.

What surprised me was that Jacob taught about being in the moment and not carrying baggage from the past. He talked about not making assumptions and not taking things personally. He talked about not gossiping. So how was it that he had listened to some gossip, taken it personally, made assumptions, and wrote to me condemning me for being ungrateful? That certainly wasn't enlightened behavior. Something was really off.

I hadn't been angry before but I was angry now. I wrote back telling him that if hell was my home, it wasn't because I wasn't grateful. Hell was my home because I was living in a community that patted itself on the back, thinking it was awake, when in fact gossip and rules of appropriate behavior had replaced truth and freedom. "I spent the first thirty-seven years of my life passionately pursuing money," I wrote, "and the last years of my life passionately pursuing enlightenment. But now I have a passion for neither. And I will breathe a sigh of relief when I finally leave Shangri-La."

He sent me a short reply that ended in, "Wake up, dear." *No, you wake up, Jacob,* I thought to myself. There was no point in responding, though. Jacob did not respond to people who were fixated (acting out of their personality and not their true self). Why should I?

Instead I prayed that I might talk to someone who would listen to my problems and who was in a position to do something about them.

12

My prayer is answered

Something was off with Jacob. Who would listen? I wasn't going to look for people, but if someone out there was open to listening, I asked that they show up. And they did.

Clarissa was the first person. She was very involved in teaching the therapy portion of Jacob's work. She was visiting Shangri-La for a couple of weeks and had asked if she could interview me for a documentary. Never one to miss an opportunity to be the center of attention, I agreed.

I had always liked Clarissa and it was nice to have her visit my home. After the interview was over, she sat back and asked me how I was enjoying Shangri-La. A light bulb went on. I could talk to her. I told her that the community felt cultish to me and that I felt Jacob was off. I showed her my e-mail exchange with him. She was horrified. "The teacher is fixated," she said. She asked my permission to share the e-mails with Shalom, one of Jacob's students who was awake and also taught therapy with her. I agreed.

Lenore and her partner were two other people whom I found I could talk to. Lenore had been the managing director of the foundation and had helped us move to Shangri-La. For some reason she had resigned several months before, but was still living in Shangri-La. One Friday night she invited me out for drinks. I was happy to meet her and her partner as I didn't often have the opportunity to socialize with them.

Not only was I very fond of Lenore, I trusted her and respected her. She was one of the few people whom I saw as a role model. She had the best qualities of both the material and spiritual world. She was smart, capable, sophisticated, an excellent manager, and at the same time she was kind, loving, with integrity and compassion. What a combination.

Over drinks she asked me how I was. I proceeded to blurt out everything that I had been holding in—the yucky behavior of the community and of Jacob. "Something is off with Jacob," I said. To my relief Lenore and her partner agreed but they didn't tell me what it was or why they were no longer working for the foundation. I would soon find out.

13

The guru falls

I was moving in three days. A friend from the spiritual community had offered to let me and the cats stay with her in Petaluma until I found work. Petaluma is a pretty little town in Sonoma about half an hour north of where I had lived in Marin. I was mostly packed and relieved that I finally knew where I was going.

My friend Sandy had invited me to dinner to say good-bye. Then suddenly she left me a mysterious phone message canceling the dinner. She said she couldn't explain but she sounded shaken up. What was going on?

At 7:30 the next morning there was a knock on my door. It was another good friend, Andrea. I had worked with Andrea and her husband, Cecil, for the foundation, and we had moved to Shangri-La together. They were both good friends to me. Cecil was away, driving the foundation's van to the site of the next retreat. Andrea no longer worked for the foundation, as she had been experiencing migraine headaches and could no longer do all the computer work that was needed.

Andrea was angry. I was surprised because she was always so calm. She sat across from me on the couch and told me that Jacob and Lakshmi had called a staff meeting. At this staff meeting Jacob confessed he had had a sexual relationship with Rachel for three years.

(Remember Jacob's enlightened student who took care of him and was no longer interested in men?)

The sexual relationship with Rachel had ended the year before when Lakshmi found out about it. Their marriage had almost ended but apparently they had made up and renewed their vows (and soon after taught a couple's retreat). This was the reason that Lenore, the managing director, and her partner had resigned. No one else knew about the affair but now Rachel was requesting that it be made public. Jacob admitted he had had an affair but he still believed he was a good teacher who could continue teaching.

His staff disagreed. Everyone who worked for Jacob resigned. His foundation was closed though Lakshmi's foundation continued. The spiritual community fell apart. Actually, I would say that many people who had worshipped Jacob finally woke up to the fact that he was human. It wasn't a pretty picture. The people who had put him on a pedestal were the angriest. Hateful e-mails were sent to him. It was heartbreaking.

I could understand the anger. People had moved to Shangri-La for him. Some had suffered financially. Some had worked for free for years for him. Of course no one had been forced to do this. In fact, people had been asked to not move to Shangri-La. I have found that when I am angry with someone, I am really angry with myself because I have committed a self-betrayal. And that's what the backlash was about.

I wasn't angry because I had already processed through my anger with Jacob. And although I hadn't known about the sexual relationship with Rachel, I knew that Jacob was no saint. He had fallen off the pedestal for me a while ago. But he had been a good teacher to me and he had offered me work when I needed it. I felt sad.

As I read the hateful e-mails sent to him, I asked myself, *Where's the compassion? Where is forgiveness? Where is love?*

I wrote an e-mail to Jacob telling him how sorry I was for the turn of events, and how grateful I was to him because he had delivered on his promise of freedom. I was free not only from the material trance but I was also free from giving my power away to him or any other teacher. And now the cult of the silent, staring, smiling people had collapsed. They were no longer silent and they certainly weren't smiling. But at least they were finally being real.

14

The victim/hero/villain triangle

And what about Rachel? Well, in Shangri-La she was considered the victim, while Jacob was considered the villain.

A friend had told me how important it is to stay out of victim/hero/villain triangles. These are relationships that are full of drama. One person is supposedly victimized by another. If you go in to save the victim, you are acting as the hero and you are in trouble, because if you play one role in this triangle, you will wind up playing all the roles. This triangle is an energy suck and these relationships go nowhere.

I realized that many of my relationships in this spiritual community were played in this arena. Sometimes I tried to help a person who was acting like a victim, thus becoming the hero. Perhaps they had run out of money and I would offer financial support. Then I wouldn't feel appreciated and I would get angry, thus becoming the villain. Or I would realize that I couldn't give any more money and the friend would get angry with me. Either way, the relationship would end and I would feel like the victim.

Sometimes I felt like a victim and wanted somebody, anybody, to help me. Someone would rush to my side to save me—for example, by offering a place for me to stay—and for a while they would be my hero. But when they started to get controlling—as people who help you often do—they became the villain. I would get angry and again the relationship would end.

This triangle was being played out in a very large karmic way in our community—with Jacob and Rachel—and for me it was a blessing. I made a commitment to myself not to get involved again in trying to save someone who was feeling like a victim. And I made a commitment to start taking responsibility for myself so that I would not feel like a victim.

In fact, there are no victims, there are no villains, and there are no heroes. We all make choices that have consequences. When we make bad choices the consequences can be very painful.

15

Manifesting a happy life

Needless to say, I was happy to leave Shangri-La behind. I was happy to leave the hateful e-mails, the angry or numb devotees, the victimized lover, the gurus, the chaos. I had already processed through much of my anger, my victimhood, and my fears. The house of cards had fallen and that was a good thing. I was not leaving a cult behind.

With two howling cats in the back of my BMW, I drove into the sunset, headed back to the Bay Area to start a new, abundant life. I spent nine months at my friend's house in Petaluma. She told me her house was very lucky. People who stayed with her and had no money always wound up leaving with abundance.

She was right. Five months after I moved to her house, I got a wonderful job offer working for a high tech company. I never thought I would work for a big corporation again but this job had everything I wanted. Before I started looking for a job, I wrote down my nine criteria:

- a desirable hourly wage
- as much work as I could handle
- using skills that I had
- easy, stress free
- no commute

- flexibility in hours
- freedom
- a boss who really appreciated me
- working with a team of people whom
  I liked and who liked me

This job had all of the above qualities and it fell into my lap. I had spent so many years trying to survive below the poverty line that it took me a while to figure out I now had abundance. I remember walking by an expensive restaurant thinking my usual thought, *Oh, I can't afford to eat there,* when I realized that I could afford to eat anywhere I wanted.

I remember bringing home stray kittens who would eat all the food I put in front of them because they hadn't realized that their lot in life had changed, and that they could have all the food that they wanted. For a while that's how I felt. It took me some time before I could be totally present in my job. The first month, as each hour went by, I heard the cash register ring $$$.

The first month I received my paycheck, which was twice the amount that I had earned the entire year before, I was ecstatic. I paid off four credit cards, took my car in for new wheels and an alignment, got a good haircut and a pedicure, bought moisturizers, makeup, some new clothes, and helped my mom. I felt like a millionaire.

The second month I paid a visit to the dentist, got myself health insurance, went to the gynecologist for a checkup, and had a blood test and looked into hormone replacement. It had been over two years since I had done any of these things.

The third month I started a savings account. I couldn't remember the last time I had savings.

By the fourth month, it was time to look for my own place. Again, I wrote down everything that I wanted in a home: old, charming house with large windows, light, French doors that opened onto a wrap-around deck, a garden that I didn't have to take care of, cat friendly, hardwood floors, built-in bookshelves—my list went on and on for two pages. Then I got on craigslist to see what rentals were available, and the second house I saw had pictures of a wrap-around deck, a garden, huge windows, and hardwood floors. I knew it was my house. I saw it the next day and in a week I had moved in.

By now you get the gist of it. The way to manifest your desires is to be clear about what you want and to feel excited as you visualize what you will be receiving. It worked with my job and it worked with my house. Now all my desires were met. I worked in my beautiful home, at my stress-free job, and started to clean up the financial mess I had created by pursuing spirituality for all these years.

I was happy with what I had, and what I had was enough. I think this may have been the first time that I experienced this feeling of satisfaction. It's funny, but I had earned as much money before when I lived in New York and when I first moved to the Bay Area. The big difference now was that I felt grateful about all I had. And I still do. Not a day goes by that I don't feel grateful for my job, for my home, for the fact that I can go to the farmer's market and buy anything I want, or that I can take my cat to the vet when he gets into a fight and needs healing.

Epilogue

Like the cat who finally realizes that she will always have plenty of food, I have finally relaxed into the material wealth that my job offers me. The bottom rung of Maslow's pyramid, with the hierarchy of needs, is being taken care of. I have food, shelter, and security (yeah, yeah, there's no such thing as security, but you know what I mean).

And friends have shown up in my life again—the need for affiliation being the second rung on the pyramid. Some are new and some are old. One thing that these friendships have in common is that they do not play in the victim/villain/hero triangle.

With these lower needs taken care of, I can now focus on self-actualization. What am I here to offer the world? How can I contribute? What are the gifts that I have been given and which gifts do I need to share? How can I show up?

It occurred to me that previously I had tried to self-actualize without having my basic needs taken care of. I thought I was above needing material security and could simply focus on spiritual enlightenment. I was wrong. Maslow's pyramid was standing on its apex and was unstable. It had to fall. But now, with a stable foundation, I can actually focus on my purpose.

And what is that? Well, it has to involve writing. Writing is something that I enjoy, that I don't feel I can even take credit for. The writing comes through me. I don't do it. When I write, I feel energized and happy. My writing has to be about spiritual topics or I'm not interested.

Since I see everything as spiritual these days, it's not difficult to find spiritual topics.

I've started writing a blog—even though right now only friends and family are reading it—because I feel that this creative energy needs to move.

I'm hoping this book will be a best seller and that it will help many people going through a similar journey. I'm hoping that someday I can support myself only by writing, as that will be the equivalent to not working for me.

Of course I have no control over any of this. All I can do is offer my story and pray that it serves.

I am so grateful that you shared this part of my journey with me.

Of course, my journey continues …

To read about my continuing journey,

please visit my blog at

http://Despina-NotAGuru.blogspot.com

Printed in the United States
137513LV00002B/10/P

9 781440 112454